TH KINGDOM

Living the Fourth Dimension

TONY SCOTT
FOREWORD BY DR. TONY STEWART

The Kingdom: Living the Fourth Dimension
© 2024 by Tony D. Scott

Unless otherwise noted, all Scripture quotations are taken from the Amplified® Bible. Copyright © 2015 by The Lockman Foundation, La Habra, CA 90631. Used by permission. www.Lockman.org.

Scripture quotations marked (TPT) are from The Passion Translation®. Copyright © 2017, 2018, 2020 by Passion & Fire Ministries, Inc. Used by permission. All rights reserved. ThePassionTranslation.com.

Scripture quotations marked (NIV) are from THE HOLY BIBLE, NEW INTERNATIONAL VERSION®, NIV®. Copyright © 1973, 1978, 1984, 2011 by Biblica, Inc.® Used by permission. All rights reserved worldwide.

Scripture quotations marked (NKJV) are from the New King James Version®. Copyright © 1982 by Thomas Nelson. Used by permission. All rights reserved.

Scripture quotations marked (MSG) are from THE MESSAGE. Copyright © 1993, 2002, 2018 by Eugene H. Peterson. Used by permission of NavPress. All rights reserved. Represented by Tyndale House Publishers, Inc.

Scripture quotation marked (KJV) is taken from the King James Version of the Bible.

Scripture quotation marked (NLT) is taken from the Holy Bible, New Living Translation. Copyright © 1996, 2004, 2015 by Tyndale House Foundation. Used by permission of Tyndale House Publishers, Inc., Carol Stream, Illinois 60188. All rights reserved.

Scripture quotations marked (AMPC) are from the Amplified® Bible (AMPC). Copyright © 1954, 1958, 1962, 1964, 1965, 1987 by The Lockman Foundation. Used by permission. www. Lockman.org.

Scripture quotations marked (AMP) are taken from the Amplified Bible, Copyright © 2015 by The Lockman Foundation. Used by permission. www.Lockman.org

Paperback ISBN: 979-8-9907770-0-2
Hardback ISBN: 979-8-9907770-1-9
E-Book ISBN: 979-8-9907770-2-6

Library of Congress Control Number: 2024910016

Printed in the United States of America.

Dedication

As the saying goes—no one lives on an island. We all depend on the people around us as we journey through life. For Shirley and I, family has always been of the utmost importance—our son, Darin, our daughter, Melony, and our four granddaughters are the crown jewels of our lives.

As challenging as life is sometimes with raising children, the blessings and the joys have outweighed the sorrows. ShirleyAnn made me what I am today. If anyone ever lived a devoted Kingdom life, it was her. Without Melony, I wouldn't be approaching 50 years of ministry. Gifted, talented, and dedicated wholly to Christ, she is a shining star in His Kingdom. She is the epitome of a Kingdom life. The future is bright, with the calling of God upon Olivia and Mackenzie to carry the legacy of ministry forward. Even as small children, it was evident that they were born with a Kingdom destiny. Without question, Darin possesses a kind, loving, and generous spirit. I'm excited to see how the Kingdom will benefit from his unique and incredible gifts. Bella and Abbie continue daily in my prayers that they will one day understand and experience the depth of our love. To all of them, I dedicate this book for the glory of the Kingdom.

Endorsements

Anyone attending a Bible-based church has heard the terms "Kingdom of God" or "Kingdom of Heaven." For most Christians, the word kingdom refers to the eternal realm, the heavenly city, the courts of Heaven, or the ministry in a local church. I was in full-time ministry for 42 years before I ever heard the Kingdom explained correctly, and when I did, my spiritual walk with God transformed. Pastor Tony Scott has the greatest and most in-depth comprehension and understanding of the true meaning and operation of the Kingdom...more than any other minister that I have ever heard teach on this subject. We always speak of the Church; however, Jesus always spoke of the Kingdom. Now you can discover the reasons why. I can promise you that your entire life is about to move into another level of spiritual breakthrough after reading and absorbing this amazing book.

> PERRY STONE, JR.
> Founder of Voice of Evangelism
> and Omega Center International

Tony Scott is uniquely positioned to write about and pass on to us the principles of living a Biblical, God-honoring life. He has been through life's fires, spent his life studying and digging into God's Word for answers to life's deepest challenges, and poured his heart out before the Throne of God, seeking His face and His ways. As our world descends further into darkness and utter nonsense and confusion, Tony reveals that when we re-center on God's identity for ourselves, instead of the world's "feelings" and identity that fulfills self, we can truly live out God's plan in our lives with an eternal focus. Like all his books, *The Kingdom: Living the Fourth Dimension* will bless your life, and you'll want to use it to bless others' lives too!

> CHAD CONNELLY
> Founder & President of Faith Wins

It has been my privilege in the past to endorse books and articles written by Tony Scott, doing so in confidence that the subject matter is well researched, anointed, and penned in a professional manner. *The Kingdom: Living the Fourth Dimension* is no exception. Scott uses his vast knowledge and ministry experience of Kingdom Living to present this timely message, which offers the opportunity to live your highest life.

BISHOP TIM HILL
Presiding Bishop/General Overseer, Church of God

In my eyes, Tony Scott is a true hero in the faith! Scott's book, *The Kingdom: Living the Fourth Dimension*, is a must-read that dives into the intricacies of daily Christian life. Through insightful discussions on valuable Kingdom concepts, Scott inspires readers to take bold action in spreading the gospel. With guidance and a message of hope, this book is a resource for believers seeking to navigate their faith journey with purpose and passion.

DINO RIZZO
Associate Pastor of Church of the Highlands

Tony Scott is passionate about his Lord and Savior and the Kingdom He leads. Tony contends that the order the Creator designed for our Universe was meant for every nation, every country, every culture, and every people group on the face of the Earth. He helps the reader see that only by living out the principles of God's Kingdom as our forefathers intended will we ever come to the place where we see the America they envisioned. Tony Scott's book *The Kingdom: Living the Fourth Dimension* presents both a challenge and an opportunity to live out those Kingdom principles and see our nation changed from the inside out.

DR. JIM GARLOW
CEO, Well Versed

This book by Tony Scott—*The Kingdom: Living the Fourth Dimension*—proves beyond a shadow of a doubt that every believer can be as close to God as they are willing to venture and that if they seek God with their whole heart, He promises to be found by them! What a powerful truth this book presents-we can live in His Kingdom in the here and now.

JENTEZEN FRANKLIN
Senior Pastor of Free Chapel

Get ready for your thinking concerning the Kingdom of God to be challenged with this new book by Tony Scott. In Paul's writings, he shares that communication by the "Spirit of the Kingdom" infuses citizens of this Kingdom with the unutterable ability to understand more than we know! This will always leave us filled with wonder and mystery that draws us to that which is always...beyond. *The Kingdom: Living the Fourth Dimension* is a record of Tony's unleashed heart of wonder and passion with the summons to engage a life beyond, through the Spirit beyond, to a sustained life in the Kingdom that is always...beyond! For those who desire spiritual life on a higher plane, this book is a must-read. It will be life-transforming.

TOM STERBENS
Lead Pastor of New Hope Church

My friend, Tony Scott, has not only penned a compelling book, *The Kingdom: Living the Fourth Dimension*—he lives it! Within its pages, you will discover laws and principles that will revolutionize your understanding of the Kingdom Jesus came to bestow upon us. For every serious seeker of God, this book is a navigational tool for embracing a Kingdom-centered life. Get it! Absorb it! Embody it! Be the Kingdom!

REVEREND SAMMY RODRIGUEZ
President of National Hispanic Christian Leadership
Conference (NHCLC)

When one looks at the world scene today, and especially as we view our own nation, it is becoming increasingly clear that we are missing some of the elements that our forefathers sowed into our founding documents. Without question, these were spiritual men who possessed a Kingdom mindset. America was intended to be a Christian nation built upon the foundation of God's Kingdom. Tony Scott has given us sincere truths about His Kingdom and how it operates. I highly recommend that you read it, study it, and live it.

BOB MCEWEN
US House of Representatives, Fmr. Member, Ohio,
Executive Director, Council for National Policy

Tony Scott is a pastor who has spent his life studying the Bible and what it means for us today. But despite decades of intense study and research, he has the remarkable ability to teach the most complex principles in a way anyone can understand. The truth is, most people have no clue about the significance of God's Kingdom, but in his new book, *The Kingdom: Living the Fourth Dimension*, he reveals just how life-changing it can be. Now, millions of people can access this amazing teaching and open up their lives to a dimension most have never dreamed of.

PHIL COOKE, PH.D.
Filmmaker, media consultant, & co-founder
of *Cooke Media Group* and *The Influence Lab*

The Kingdom: Living the Fourth Dimension is a compelling and insightful read into the power for living an authentic Christian life. Pastor Tony Scott has tapped into the core essential truths to the victorious Spirit-filled life that's available to all people. This is a must-read for anyone who desires to fully experience the Kingdom of God in everyday life.

MARK WALKER
President of Lee University

In *The Kingdom: Living the Fourth Dimension,* Tony Scott challenges us to wake up and truly live the life God has designed for us. This book offers practical insights and Biblical wisdom that will equip any believer to see beyond human potential and tap into a spirit-empowered life. I have no doubt every person who opens the pages of this book will be inspired to a measure of greater surrender and benefit from discovering their uniqueness in Christ.

JOE DOBBINS
Lead Pastor of Twin Rivers Church

The Holy Spirit has enabled Tony Scott to skillfully put some of the best insights into the Kingdom I have ever read. His book reveals decades of study, prayer, and pastoral experience that come out of his heart with scriptural clarity. He has said what I have been trying to say my entire ministry.

LORAN LIVINGSTON
Senior Pastor of the Charlotte Central Church of God

The powerful message of freedom woven through *The Kingdom: Living the Fourth Dimension* emphasizes the importance of aligning with God's Kingdom laws for true liberation. Tony Scott articulates how failure to tap into these laws limits life's potential while embracing them empowers individuals to live a God-filled life. The vision of an ever-expanding and victorious Kingdom encourages readers to live according to these divine principles.

This book is a profound guide for those seeking a deeper understanding of their God-given identity and purpose. The call to continually advance the Kingdom cause resonates as a source of energy, passion, and fulfillment. It challenges readers to reflect on their availability to God's Kingdom and invites them into a life of alignment with His transformative laws. A must-read for those on a journey of spiritual discovery and Kingdom living.

KEN WRIGHT
Founder & Senior Pastor of Life Point Church

If you're ready to understand and experience the "supernatural life" that's been made available to believers today, then this hard-to-put-down book by Tony Scott is a must-read! He is a gift to the body of Christ and has masterfully wrapped 50 years of pastoral study and experience into this deep, yet practical guide to living the Kingdom life we as believers have been promised by God. Get ready to be encouraged, inspired, and emboldened to pursue the life that God has made available to you!

> SCOTT SHEPPARD
> Lead Pastor at Cornerstone Church

Everything in the Kingdom of God is diametrically opposed and mutually exclusive of everything in the kingdom of darkness. God has called you out of darkness to live in His marvelous light. The problem with many people is that they accept the call into God's Kingdom while continuing to live according to the principles of the kingdom of darkness. One issue is that many in the western world, especially those who live in nations with representative governments, are unfamiliar with kingdom concepts. Many believers consider Kingdom living to be complicated and unachievable. In his book *The Kingdom: Living the Fourth Dimension,* Tony Scott explains Kingdom principles with clarity and authority. Your life doesn't have to be normal and nominal. This book will help you understand, internalize, and activate Kingdom truths that will propel you to a life of satisfaction, effectiveness, and fulfillment in the Kingdom of God.

> DR. ROD PARSLEY
> Pastor and Founder of World Harvest Church /
> Breakthrough Media Ministries

Contents

Foreword

The Challenge for Fourth Dimension Living

THE central message of the ministry of Jesus was Kingdom living for all believers. Throughout the Gospels, we read accounts of how He taught His disciples and followers with these instructions. Thousands of years later, Jesus' teachings are more alive than ever and serve as guidelines of inspiration for the modern believer.

Prophecies in the Old Testament foretold the coming of the Messiah and the New Testament describes the life of Jesus that consistently preaches an unwavering Kingdom message. Jesus even specifically instructs us to pray in Matthew 6:10: "Thy Kingdom come, thy will be done on Earth as it is in Heaven" (KJV).

From the beginning and through his many years of rich ministry, Tony Scott has taught and preached a Kingdom message. In his new book, *The Kingdom–Living the Fourth Dimension*, he uses inspired detail to encapsulate how to have a Kingdom life as he adopts the simplicity of the ministry of Jesus to move us to another dimension of living.

Tony Scott's book challenges us to embrace living beyond the accepted norm, beyond the "three dimensions" the world offers us.

As members of God's Kingdom, we have access to more than just the secular interpretation of success, but an anointed and proven formula for living our best life in the power of the Holy Spirit.

For those who are searching, the context of his book not only describes the experience but also offers guidelines to embrace victorious living in the Fourth Dimension.

TONY D. STEWART
Assistant General Overseer
Church of God
Cleveland, TN

Why This Book?

IN today's world, there has occurred a global pandemic, Russia's bombardment of Ukraine, Hamas' attempt to destroy the nation of Israel, and the possibility of World War III. As a result, many people are anxious and **feeling on edge.**

Aware of these challenges and others, Tony Scott, a pastor of some fifty years, has written a book about God's Kingdom—*The Kingdom: Living the Fourth Dimension.* In his book, he does not claim to know what the future holds, but for him, the Bible reveals that the sovereign God has His hands on all the challenges facing God's people in the present and future.

The rule of God's Kingdom includes all believers and extends beyond the church. God's reign is first and foremost about the salvation of people (John 3:5-7) and that God has dominion over the hearts and lives of those who willingly submit to His lordship. The basic and necessary requirements are repentance and the new birth, which enable people to enter the Kingdom and prepare them for the world to come.

The Kingdom of God has a number of facets, including being God-centered, universal, present, future, and powerful. The future bliss of the Kingdom will be realized in the millennial reign of Christ on the Earth. But in the meantime, until Christ comes the second time, God's rule and grace will continue to work in the spiritual and social realms, opposing violence, injustice, and demonic powers— every form of evil. Ultimately and finally, "the God of Heaven will set up a Kingdom which shall never be destroyed" (Daniel 2:44).

Scott's main focus is on the present facet of the reign of God. *The Kingdom: Living the Fourth Dimension* is written in clear language, and its message is practical and pastoral, dealing with matters and challenges of daily Christian living. The book consists of eight chapters, and once you begin reading it, it is hard to put down. Throughout it, you will observe that Scott allows the Bible to speak for itself. Also, out of the passion of his heart, he explains the meaning of the Gospel to anyone who needs salvation, encouragement, exhortation, and instruction. Those who read and study this book will be spiritually enriched. It is a message of guidance and hope for believers.

FRENCH L. ARRINGTON, PH.D., DD
Professor of New Testament Greek and Exegesis
and of the Niko Njotorahardjo Chair of
the Restoration of the Tabernacle of David
at the Pentecostal Theological Seminary

Introduction

YOU have a Kingdom identity—discover it and live it. It was given to you by God in Genesis 1:26. You are created in His image after His likeness. Perhaps this is the most profound statement about your human worth and value in God's eyes. Your true God-self is found within your human spirit.

> *"Nor will people say, 'Look! Here [it is]!' or, 'See, [it is] there!' For behold, the Kingdom of God is within you [in your hearts] and among you [surrounding you]" (Luke 17:21 AMPC).*

Since His Kingdom is within each of us, we must spend our lives searching for it at the core of our beings. A Kingdom perspective in my daily life causes me to seek His Kingdom continuously (Matthew 6:33). Perhaps we refer to this as life in **Living the Fourth Dimension**—life beyond spirit, soul, body.

Nowhere in the New Testament does Jesus command us to build a church—actually, He said, *"I will build My Church."* We are simply commanded to preach the liberating Gospel of the Kingdom—not the gospel of the Church *(Luke 4:43).*

Everywhere man is born free; however, he creates his own bondage and chains. True freedom comes as a result of God's Kingdom Laws being sown into the very spirit of man. Freedom works best when it heeds the voice of conscience, or else it becomes the enemy of humanity and culture.

Failure to tap into His Kingdom laws is one of the most limiting factors in life. His Kingdom laws, when obeyed, empower us to dominate and rule in life. His Kingdom is ever-expanding, ever-becoming, ever-empowering, ever-victorious. Man's total restoration and surrender to God can only be accomplished by knowing and living His Kingdom laws. As you live them, you see the world from God's perspective. Living Kingdom laws brings the highest and best use of your life.

When you are continually advancing His Kingdom cause, your life is filled with energy, passion, and fulfillment.

His Kingdom is available to you.
Are you available to His Kingdom?

The Kingdom:
Your Highest Life

Are you living your highest life?

EVERYONE born is affected by two lives—their lived and unlived life. Your getting up, getting ready, going to school, going to work—whatever you do each day—entails your **lived life**. Your **unlived life** is what is inside of you—dreams, hopes, aspirations, thoughts, desires—which, to this point, you have never lived. God designed His Kingdom to pull out of your inner being everything He created you to be. He wants you to live your unlived life more than you want to live it.

Life happens to you as you live. Circumstances, conflicts, and challenges are part of your life, but they should not define it. We're talking about real life as God designed it.

Life as God intended.
Life to the ultimate degree.
Life with a capital "L."

The question is: Will you really live before you die?

Kingdom life is the highest possible life strategy. The Good News of His Kingdom message is that all of God's power is now available to break into our mundane, monotonous Christian lives with His victory, energy, and passion.

According to His Word, the supreme purpose of our lives is to know Jesus and to be known by Him. The Christian life is an adventure involving the **quest**, the **pursuit**, and the **search for His Kingdom**.

You and I live in **the world of doing**; the **Kingdom is the world of being**. We are eternal creatures. Ecclesiastes 3:11 says God has placed "*eternity in our hearts.*" Obviously, we have lost the sense of eternal living while here. All of us are aware of **something more** than this transient world. **Eternity** refers to the future—a longing or sense of eternity, an innate knowledge that there is far more than we are experiencing in the here and now.

God designed us so we cannot be completely apart from this **eternity**. God cannot be God unless He is eternal—meaning no beginning and no ending. He alone has uncreated life. We all come with a God-chip—GPS (God Positioning System). Eternity refers to our deep and abiding awareness of something outside the boundaries of our five senses. It is the arena of your spiritual being, which happened at the very beginning of your life in your mother's womb. As the sperm met the egg, an embryo was created and accompanied by a flash of bright light. Literally, that is God's uncreated life entering your created life.

We are created **eternal creatures** but have lost sight of **eternal living**. Spiritual formation is training in eternal living, intentional discipleship to Jesus, and the method by which we discover the renewable source of spiritual life-energy we are searching for. Our sense of eternity brings **fulfillment** and **satisfaction**, and our purpose is thus experienced.

Church, Christian living, serving, praying, and singing can get monotonous and repetitious. However, from the beginning, God assigned the human job description. We are to rule collectively over all living things on Earth—animals and plants. We are responsible before God for life on Earth. God equipped us with a purpose by creating us to function in a conscious, personal covenant relationship of interactive responsibility with Him.

We have tasted the powers of the age to come.

"Once people have seen the light, gotten a taste of Heaven and been part of the work of the Holy Spirit, once they've personally experienced the sheer goodness of God's Word and the powers breaking in on us..." (Hebrews 6:4-5 MSG).

So once again, the question for all of us is:

*Are you living the life God **designed for you**
and **designed you for**?*

The Kingdom of God is the rule, the reign, the government of God in the lives of those who are surrendered to His lordship. Nothing is more important to your life than knowing, experiencing, and living the laws of His Kingdom. From the beginning, man has had the option of living in a **Creation covenant** with God. Human beings are assigned the rule over all living things and to be responsible to God for life on Earth.

However, we must experience a personal, intimate, interactive relationship with Jesus and invest the totality of our being into Him and His Kingdom. **We need this Kingdom life—our souls long for it.** There is something about this life that causes us to transcend into the **Fourth Dimension**. Beyond physical existence, God's Word offers life on a higher level through His Kingdom.

We should know and understand six things about His Kingdom:

You can be near the Kingdom.

The Kingdom has come close to you (Luke 10:9).

You can see the Kingdom.

Unless a person is born again, he can never see the Kingdom of God (John 3:3).

You can enter the Kingdom.

Unless a man is born of water and the Spirit, he cannot enter the Kingdom of God (John 3:5).

You can receive the Kingdom.

Do not be seized with alarm and struck with fear, little flock, for it is your Father's good pleasure to give you the Kingdom (Luke 12:32).

You can possess the Kingdom.

The Kingdom of Heaven has endured violent assault, and violent men seize it by force (Matthew 11:12).

You can be possessed by the Kingdom.

The Kingdom of God is within you and among you (Luke 17:21).

His Kingdom is manifested in and through you—an invitation for a spiritual journey into the heart and life of God Himself. God intended our behaviors to be a pure expression of His divine nature through us. **Godliness is His capacity to reproduce Himself in and through you. Your inability never diminishes His ability.**

The primary demand of the Kingdom is a response of man's will to receive it, to yield to its control, and to pursue it. Living by Kingdom laws, we manifest the Kingdom and make Kingdom disciples!

By imparting to us and conferring upon us a Kingdom, Jesus arranged for the delivery of His life into us. Only by living the

Kingdom life can we understand our reasons for being here. We live in a "crazy world" today. **Confusion abounds.** A culture of busyness and noise surrounds us.

In our physical, daily lives, we are constantly doing something. There must be activity; we must be viewing something, listening to something. Through the process of "doing" in the physical life, we create feelings from what we are doing, and out of that, we become. **We think "doing" actually creates our lives.** We believe that out of all that doing, we develop feelings and then become.

In the spiritual life, **you first become, and then you develop your feelings out of becoming.** Your life comes out of who you have become. You must develop who you are in Christ, which brings true spiritual feelings, and out of that, you "do."

Natural life = doing $\Rightarrow$ feeling $\Rightarrow$ becoming

Spiritual life = becoming $\Rightarrow$ feeling $\Rightarrow$ doing

We are spiritual beings living in an unspiritual world. When we get caught up in the world of doing, we are caught up in our flesh—mind, will, and emotions. **Doing** from the **natural side** does not complete you or fulfill you. First, **you must become your true spiritual self and then live out your true Kingdom life.** Those feelings will boost your boldness and your spirit of adventure. Your "doing" is now out of who you have become.

The world sees you as body, soul, spirit.
In the Kingdom, you are spirit, soul, body.

We **see** the Kingdom as we are born into it, and we live in Him. As many have experienced, we are created with a God-designed purpose and equipped to function in a conscious, personal relationship of interactive responsibility.

In the Garden, He assigned a **Kingdom mandate** to Adam and

Eve—to guard, keep, and tend it. He does the same thing to us in a Kingdom way. He said, *"I am conferring upon you a Kingdom, and My life flows in and through you. You will produce Kingdom results for the world to see, as you depend upon My Holy Spirit"* (*Luke 22:29*). This comes from a personal relationship with Him. His Presence will go before you to mark out the way.

God is constantly interacting and flowing His life through us.

"I have been crucified with Christ [in Him I have shared His crucifixion]; it is no longer I who live, but Christ (the Messiah) lives in me; and the life I now live in the body I live by faith in (by adherence to and reliance on and complete trust in) the Son of God, Who loved me and gave Himself up for me" (*Galatians 2:20 AMPC*).

God is forever communicating His will for His children on Earth. **We have the opportunity to tune into a spiritual realm where we hear and know His voice.** He says, *"The sheep that are My own hear and are listening to My voice; and I know them, and they follow Me"* (*John 10:27 AMPC*). God is always speaking and saying something. The atmosphere is filled with the knowledge of God. When we are praying and intersecting with that knowledge, then **we have a manifestation of His Kingdom.**

In our atmosphere, there are AM and FM radio waves, as well as satellite signals. With the proper equipment, you can pick those up and hear what is said. As you join Him in what He is doing, you enjoy the interactive, personal relationship He designed you for. As you listen to this voice and focus on Him, you experience the fullness of the Kingdom life. The moment your living intersects with what He's speaking and doing, there is a manifestation of the Kingdom. You are now "doing" out of who He has made you to become for His Kingdom's sake.

"For we are God's [own] handiwork (His workmanship), recreated in Christ Jesus, [born anew] that we may do those good works which God predestined (planned beforehand) for us [taking paths which He prepared ahead of time], that we should walk in them [living the good life which He prearranged and made ready for us to live]" (Ephesians 2:10 AMPC).

He's already designed works for us. And He's already designed us for those works. It's a two-fold thing. When we go after Him and His Presence, it's not to plead our cases. The purpose is for God to speak to us about His ways—how He wants us to live. We should get quiet in His Presence to focus on His words to us.

What we have lost in this generation is the power of true **spiritual meditation** where we do like David, who said: *"While I was musing—thinking deep, hot thoughts of God—the fire began to burn" (Psalm 39:3).* Passion comes out of the deep, intense focus of your emotions upon the matter at hand. It grips you on the inside and comes to the outside. You become more intense, focused, and driven by a fire from within. God and His Kingdom are not add-ons. His Kingdom life is your true life—**your unlived life.**

Let's look at the beginning of Creation. The initial thought behind marriage was to allow Adam and Eve to complement one another. Adam was created, and God built Eve to complete his life. Through the process of doing that, she completes herself and becomes who she truly is. Every woman has the possibility of experiencing life as a daughter, sister, friend, wife, mother, grandmother, and counselor. Eve had the fullest expression of her being through Adam because she came from him. Likewise, by becoming one with God and achieving that unique **oneness relationship**, He releases you to become who you truly are. Then, you can "do" out of who you have "become."

Adam and Eve were created as perfect human beings. They had already "become." As long as they were "doing," according to God's command, they were fulfilled. God says, "You have become like I made you (image); now go and live like Me (likeness)." When they ate from the Tree of Knowledge of Good and Evil, their flesh enticed them to "do" something to "become." Satan said, "You eat from this tree, and you will **become** like God." When they began to stray from His commands, they were no longer complete in themselves. They were lost. When you become a true child of God, what you feel and do are out of **who** you have become.

Daily, we are bombarded with messages about living our best lives—get this, try this, use this, do this, and you will become the best version of yourself. But through the process of becoming who God created you to be, you open your life up to the **God-designed, God-assigned** person He created you to become. **We become whole, well, and complete only as we come to know and experience God and His Kingdom and live by His laws, rules, and principles.**

He fills our lives with favor, blessings, and power as we willingly submit to Him. He involves us in His **Kingdom exploits** as we seek first His Kingdom and His righteousness. *"...And have felt how good the Word of God is and the mighty **powers of the age and world to come**" (Hebrews 6:5 AMPC).*

Jesus did **three** things on Earth concerning His Kingdom:

He **proclaimed the availability** of His Kingdom to everyone.

"'All the preliminaries have been taken care of,' He said, 'And the rule of God is now accessible to everyone. Review your plans for living and base your life on this remarkable new opportunity'" (Mark 1:15 Literal Translation).

He taught **the message of His Kingdom.**

"...I must preach the Good News (the Gospel) of the Kingdom of God to the other cities [and towns] also, for I was sent for this [purpose]" (Luke 4:43 AMPC).

He **manifested His Kingdom Presence** in a way that could only be explained supernaturally.

"But if it is by the Spirit of God that I drive out demons, then the Kingdom of God has come upon you" (Matthew 12:28 NIV).

When His Kingdom life fills you, and you yield to it and submit to it, it will begin to produce a **violent burst** of life that breaks out into new dimensions of faith and power. The advancement of His Kingdom depends upon how much you allow His Kingdom power to rule you. The degree to which you live out of your human spirit— your unlived life—makes this possible.

Jesus declares a powerful principle of life that accompanies the new Kingdom era in *Matthew 11:11 (AMPC).*

"Truly I tell you, among those born of women, there has not risen anyone greater than John the Baptist; yet he who is least in the Kingdom of Heaven is greater than he."

John the Baptist is great, but those who enter His Kingdom have **more** going for them. He was someone *"with a Word from God, yet he was **more** than a prophet."* He was a "fulfilled prophecy." He not only had a "Word"—the "Word" **happened** in and through him.

Kingdom people not only have God's Word, but the "Word" happens in and through them by His Spirit.

"And from the days of John the Baptist until the present time, the Kingdom of Heaven has endured violent assault, and violent men seize it by force [as a precious prize – a share in the heavenly Kingdom is sought with most ardent zeal and intense exertion]" (Matthew 11:12 AMPC).

The word **violent** comes from a root word, from which we get our word *biology*—the science of life. The Holy Spirit's infusion of God into our lives releases Kingdom power into the world. In the natural world, it's the picture of a tree root growing under a large piece of concrete. Though the root weighs significantly less than the concrete, its life within will force the concrete upwards. The same is true with us. As we release His Kingdom power, a **violent force** of His life flows through us, powerfully affecting our challenges. When we submit **who** and **where** we are to God, then our **rules** or **dominions** increase according to the force of His Kingdom power released through us.

You and I are created as spiritual beings—literally, spirit-beings. Within each of us is a piece of the divine that longs for connection to, knowledge of, and intimacy with God. Only as we experience Kingdom life can we grasp the meaning and purpose of human existence. This Kingdom is **transcendent** and **eminent.** It transcends this world, and yet it permanently pervades and sustains it. Christ is here in the midst of His Kingdom (which is within us), ready to rule in any and all of our circumstances.

> *"Nor will people say, Look! Here [it is]! or, See, [it is] there! For behold, the Kingdom of God is within you [in your hearts] and among you [surrounding you]" (Luke 17:21 AMPC).*

You and I are made to live as Kingdom subjects, under Kingdom laws and authority, and in obedience to the commands of our King. We are created to live as spiritual beings in the spiritual environment of His Kingdom rule. His command to us is to *"seek first"* His Kingdom and His righteousness *(Matthew 6:33).* We are to pray, *"Your Kingdom come, Your will be done on Earth as it is in Heaven" (Matthew 6:10).* When we live as Kingdom subjects, speak a Kingdom message, teach Kingdom laws, and model Kingdom behavior, the world will see the difference. Any person, place, or thing fully surrendered to God's rule will experience His Kingdom's power.

Once you enter His Kingdom, you decide how close you live to the King. The closer you live to the King, the more Kingdom authority you manifest.

**Your challenges in life should never limit you—
you should limit your challenges by manifesting
Kingdom power.**

Whether or not one is a religious person, it is a fact that all of us are spiritual. Spirit is the aspect of us that you cannot see, put your finger on, hold, or handle; and yet, it is more real than your fleshly being.

Perhaps one of life's most sobering moments is when you realize something about yourself that you don't understand. You are unique; **you are essential**. Life has meaning, and it is worth living. Without understanding the **Fourth Dimension**, you cannot grasp the **why** of life.

"He has made everything beautiful in its time. He also has planted eternity in men's hearts and minds [a divinely implanted sense of a purpose working through the ages which nothing under the sun but God alone can satisfy..." (Ecclesiastes 3:11 AMPC).

He created us to **thrive**, to be fulfilled, and to be complete to the degree that we willingly surrender to His will and purpose for us. His plans call for each of us to yield our lives totally into His hands and to receive the fullness of His Holy Spirit, which then manifests itself with explosive Kingdom life.

Kingdom life, the **Fourth Dimension**, is the absolute apex— the highest life strategy. God desires us to live in and through Him, becoming who we will be forever. We were created to count, matter, and experience our value as human beings. Each of us is placed in a strategic, specific context in life to make a difference.

The deepest longings of our hearts confirm our innate calling. God assigns us to rule over the circumstances of our lives, whatever they may be. **You and I are more than just forgiven**. We are to live an eternal kind of life. Right now, we are called upon to intimately **interact** with the God of the Universe.

All of us learn how to live from our interactions with others. Our learning either limits us or releases us to increase and grow. I am not my "own person." People, circumstances, and stuff have shaped my life in ways that differ significantly from the intended purpose of my designed life.

Who or what has shaped your thinking?

"Rethink your life in the light of the fact that the Kingdom of the heavens is now open to all" (Matthew 4:17 Literal Translation).

God intended our behaviors to be a **pure expression** of His **divine nature**. Our human natures are supernaturally transformed by the infilling of His Kingdom life. As we sojourn upon the Earth, eternity makes us aware that we are intended for another world. There is a sense in which you will never feel at home here.

We all desire to know the purpose and reason for our births. **Who** did God mean when He meant me?

> ***What does God require of me,***
> ***and how does He want to use me to***
> ***make a difference in my world?***

Each day I wake up, I am given the gift of life. To pay for that life,

I must live as a Kingdom subject expressing Him in my behavior. The Kingdom of God is the heart of God. His Kingdom governs all the events of history, our daily lives, and circumstances. To the degree that His Kingdom life, the **Fourth Dimension**, fills and dominates your life, you rule in life's circumstances by the power of His Spirit.

The Kingdom's sheer force removes all limitations on God's intended purpose for us. It is big, broad, and beyond our wildest imaginations. Its fullness can never be experienced, its resources can never be depleted, and its reign is never finished. It absolutely has no boundaries. When you and I become subjects in His Kingdom, He rules our lives. The Kingdom is within and with us in a 360-degree dimension. **Living the Fourth Dimension** requires a Kingdom covenant commitment, willful obedience, and constant preparedness to live by its laws.

Ancient Kingdom wisdom teaches us that life begins with God. At this moment, no one—science, the medical field, or philosophers—has come up with a better, more reasonable explanation for the beginning of life. Even the most staunch evolutionists are stumped with the question of where life began. To this very day, they have no answer to this question. Scientists believe in **biogenesis,** which means **life can only come from life**. Our lives came from God; thus, life did not come from the evolutionary theory of a "big bang." Our only hope of understanding our identities, our purposes, and our destinies is the God Who is our lives. We are like the Source from whence we came.

Choices, decisions, motives, and intentions must all be directed to what God wants for us. Literally, we build a life foundation on God's Truth and wisdom. Our trust in Him causes us to move beyond our own understanding and wisdom to embrace His. That trust leads us into a covenant relationship with God and with others.

In today's world, the word **trust** seems to be missing as we interact with the new world order. Trust means being secure without fear, lying helpless face down. It is a picture of a servant waiting for his command in readiness to obey. Trust begins with commitment, which produces changes in our behaviors so that we can become like Him. We experience an awe of reverence, intimacy, and obligation, which marks healthy relationships. In this new way of living, He directs our paths and empowers us to walk out His will. In our regular, mundane, sometimes monotonous, everyday lives, He graces us with His Presence.

Living the Fourth Dimension results in spiritual, mental, and physical health that is thriving and radiant with wellness. We are healthy from the inside to the outside—total personal prosperity. You can also refer to it as **whole-life stewardship**—perfectly integrated into why we are here.

For you and I to live the **Pro-God life**, we must go beyond ourselves and stop living a "Pro-Tony, Pro-Mary, Pro-Joe" life. To know "who" and "why" we are requires an intimate personal relationship with Jesus. When we are self-actualized—living for a purpose and cause beyond ourselves—we become filled with His joy and powerfully alive. We are **Living the Fourth Dimension.**

We don't have to ask for His **provision when we abide continuously in His Presence**. When we give Him our first, our best—that which has value and is costly—He then releases His best into us. At that moment, we become self-actualized into our full spiritual beings. We must begin the process of experiencing "first things first"—prioritizing our lives around our true God-selves.

Daily, two powerful Kingdom laws affect our lives:
the **Law of Focus**
and the **Law of Expectation.**

The **Law of Focus** says that whatever you focus on, you will see more of it. You will also be blinded from seeing other options and choices. What you focus on expands and magnifies. When you focus on positive things, you put your mind in a pragmatic direction. Total focus will bring all three of you—spirit, soul, body—into perfect harmony and significantly impact your **Fourth Dimension Life.** The more of the five senses you bring into an experience, the greater the impact upon your life. Your sixth sense—the sense of eternity— the **Fourth Dimension**—takes you beyond the arena of your five senses.

Positive focus is liberating and unlimited. Negative focus imprisons and limits you. **Broken focus is one of mankind's greatest curses.** Focus creates and intensifies desire. Intensified desire produces energy and creativity. Focus determines direction. The mind leads, and the body follows. Focus creates reality.

Focus is always a choice of your will. When you think enough positive thoughts, your mind gradually shifts to a **Positive Operating System** that you alone can turn on. Researchers tell us that the average person speaks to himself/herself 50,000 times daily, and 80% of our self-talk is negative. You can change your focus by changing what you say to yourself and others. Words have a powerful impact on the direction of your energies.

The **Law of Expectation** says that 85% of what we fully expect to happen happens. Expectation is connected to your **Personal Belief System**. Inside each of us is a hidden secret life waiting to be released (unlived life) in the context of our expectations. Favor, blessing, happiness, and significance are ours in direct proportion to a positive **Personal Belief System** based on Kingdom principles.

Expectation Theory says we spend our whole lives becoming conditioned to expect certain stimuli to activate a learned response.

Scientists have discovered that we respond to what the brain, based on previous experience, expects to happen. Through a lifetime's worth of events, our brains learn what to expect next—whether it eventually happens that way or not—positive or negative.

As you replace old negative expectations in your mind with more positive ones, you start to believe that what you want is possible. Your brain takes over the job of accomplishing that possibility for you, thus negating your learned expectations.

High expectations, fully embraced, will cause you to surmount any obstacle and live a "no-limits" life. This is life at its highest dimension—the **Fourth Dimension**—which is exciting, fulfilling, and **causes you to discover the deepest realm of your being— your unlived life**. Here, you become fully you, fully actualized.

We are never-ceasing spiritual beings with a unique and personal eternal calling to count for good as we sojourn the Earth. We were created by God and given a **creation covenant** to rule over all living things on Earth—animals and plants. We are meant to "exercise our rule" only in union with Him as He works through us. He desires to be our constant companion and co-worker in the creative enterprise of life on Earth. Through this process, **we are becoming who we will be forever.**

When His Word is internalized within our spirits, it brings a release of Kingdom provision, resulting in:

- **The release of captives**
- **The recovery of sight to the blind**
- **The deliverance from oppression**
- **The healing in spirit, soul, body**
- **The restoration of peace**
- **The provision of every need**

Living the Fourth Dimension is filled with absolute Kingdom abundance. You and I may enjoy total favor with the Ruler of that abundance. There is never a lack of two powerful principles: **love** and **hope**. Both energize our lives and keep us on the cutting edge of what God wants to do with and through us. No life can ever be meaningful and fulfilling without experiencing these powerful virtues. Doing the "**Kingdom Thing**" means doing life His way, as God accomplishes His perfect will through us. According to Jesus' teachings, His Kingdom will reign supreme on this Earth and in Heaven.

How does the Kingdom work in the here and now?

In His Kingdom, we are **transformed** (change of form) so we can **transcend** (go beyond ordinary limitations and circumstances) and become **transparent** (let the light of Christ be seen in us), which causes us to experience **transference** (to stand in a new place).

As you experience God's love and redeeming grace, you transcend your limitations and abilities and thus transform others as they view your transformation.

Life in the Kingdom begins with prayer. Don't get caught up in cultural shallowness or become carried away with emotions and passions. Maintain **spiritual disciplines**. Stay balanced in your living—no wild mood swings. Whatever happens, don't lose your head or your faith. Don't be overcome with worry, anxiety, and fear. In the Kingdom, either you trust and pray, or you faint.

"...men ought always to pray, and not to faint" (Luke 18:1 KJV).

Prayer is not monologue but dialogue. Prayer is a process. Don't just speak to God, but listen to Him. When we pray, it's not just so God can hear us, but it's so we will hear God. As we hear His voice, we can experience **divine alignment** with His **assignment** in the Kingdom on Earth.

In the **Fourth Dimension**, you also love **fervently**. Love makes all the other virtues what they should be. Love is a choice of the will. **Fervent** describes the stretching of a muscle to its limits, thus producing maximum output. It is the picture of a galloping horse whose legs are fully extended. We are to "stretch ourselves out," fully extend, and love with maximum effort.

This kind of love covers a "multitude of sins" (1 Peter 4:8).

Focused love causes our hearts to be tender and generous toward those in need. Our fervent love for another person often blinds us to their faults. We give practical help to anyone who needs it, giving to those who can do nothing in return for us. This is to be done without complaint, without grumbling, as we use our gifts to serve others.

Because of these special spiritual endowments, given to us by the Holy Spirit,

I become **"who"** He says I am.

I am safe, secure, and protected there.

Peace rules in my heart.

Joy fills my soul.

Energy floods my being.

Living the Fourth Dimension is good!

It is there that I become who I will be forever. "To be, or not to be, that is the question" (Shakespeare).

It is my **unlived life** that determines **who** I really am.

"I have been crucified with Christ [in Him I have shared His crucifixion]; it is no longer I who live, but Christ (the Messiah) lives in me; and the life I now live in the body I live by faith in (by adherence to and reliance on and complete trust in) the Son of God, Who loved me and gave Himself up for me" (Galatians 2:20 AMPC).

Perhaps that is also Paul's thinking as he sorts through his thoughts on life and death. To him, real life means knowing, loving, serving, glorifying, enjoying, and communing with Christ. For him, Christ is his life. **Victory** is the normal Christian experience—defeat is abnormal. It is God's will that every Christian should be *"more than a conqueror."* Christ died for us so that He could live through us. We are crucified with Him so that we can live through Him. He becomes our strength. We live, fight, pray, and worship from a position of **victory**. Victory is a person—Jesus Christ. **Victory is Jesus living through the life God designed for me and designed me for**. Victory is a gift—not a reward.

Isaiah 40:31 says, "But those who wait for the Lord shall renew their strength..." (AMPC).

Renew has the meaning of **exchange**. They that wait upon the Lord shall "exchange" their strength. God offers you an **Exchanged Life**, a "substituted life" (your unlived life). I don't have to toil and struggle to produce this life—He produces it through me as I live surrendered to His will. Godliness is His nature produced through me.

Christ reveals three forms of unwearied strength through us as we face life's challenges:

Strength to **soar**.
Strength to **run**.
Strength to **walk**.

"But those who wait upon GOD get fresh strength. They spread their wings and soar like eagles, they run and don't get tired, they walk and don't lag behind" (Isaiah 40:31 MSG).

In the world's view, you would walk, run, and soar. In the **Fourth Dimension**, where you live the Exchanged Life, you **soar**, **run**, then **walk**. There is a huge difference. Regardless of your challenges, you should not cease to walk out your faith. When we are young in the Lord, we are full of zeal, excitement, and fire burning within.

Time, trials, and challenges take a toll on our passions and often weaken our faiths. But when we live the Exchanged Life, He sends seasons of refreshing (Acts 3:19) to fan the smoking embers into a flame. He strengthens us to soar—to fly like an eagle. He gives us the strength to run. Crises confront us to slow our pace and interfere with progress. In the stress, strain, and exertion to "keep on going," He strengthens us to *"run and not be weary."* When our dreams are crushed, and we are called upon to "not give up," He provides the greatest strength—*"to walk and not grow faint."*

How do we receive this gift of the Exchanged Life? It comes to those who "wait upon the Lord." Waiting is not a state of inactivity. It is a state of dependency. We actively live surrendered to His will whether we see or experience the answer, the solution. We wait in obedience. To "wait on" is another term for service. To "wait upon the Lord" is to continue living His life of victory, power, peace, and rest—not our lives of fear, anxiety, struggle, pain, and disappointment.

Whatever comes our way, we must not allow it to hinder, interfere with, or stop His life flowing through us. Keep on singing, keep on serving, keep on giving, keep on showing up, and you will be strengthened as you live the **Exchanged Life.**

Approach life each day with this mantra:

Wake up!
Get up!
Show up!

Remember that you are always **chosen, changed,** and **charged.**

THIS is real, authentic, genuine life—God-style.

When it comes to God's Kingdom, "who" we are is more

foundational and crucial than "what" we do. Our **person** is more important than our **performance**. When God chose Abram (meaning "exalted father") to create a new nation of people, He gave him a new name: Abraham ("father of a multitude"). "Israel" (meaning "clinging to God") refers to God's covenant people. Every son and daughter has an identity given to us by God.

While we live here on Earth, God forever tries to reveal who we are. He does this through the spirit of eternity He placed within our hearts. Our covenant lives are revealed as we live surrendered to His will and purpose. To live **surrendered** means constant communion with God, complete devotion to His plan, obedient service to His Kingdom, and a worship lifestyle in thought, word, and deed. **Surrendered** means Jesus is the informing and governing principle of our lives.

Paul believed that when he was born again, he received the life of Jesus into his very being. He says, "I am crucified with Christ," I no longer live as Paul.

When Christ is fully in our lives, we no longer live **self-centered,** but now we live **Christ-centered**. He shows up in my thought life, speech, actions, and how I respond to daily life. I live by faith in Him. I don't live in fear of circumstances, challenges, or trials. I try, and I fail. I trust, and He succeeds. When I, in faith, trust Him no matter what I am facing, He releases His life through me. He is limited only by the measure of our **availability** to all that He makes available to us.

Our greatest ability—**availability**.

When we are surrendered to Him, everything that is possible to Him becomes possible to us. Literally, we live a **Him-possible** life.

When you are **Christ-inhabited**, you will be **Christ-sustained,** and you will be **Christ-strengthened**. When fully surrendered, I am not interfering with His work in and through me. Every day, we need 220 volts of power in our lives (Galatians 2:20).

This sign once hung in a dry cleaning and fabric dyeing business:

We dye to live;
We live to dye;
The more we dye, the more we live;
And the more we live, the more we dye.

God's covenant people are here on Earth for the specific purpose of living a life we are not capable of living so that our living reveals Him.

Despite all that surrounds us today: terrorism, economic distress, godless living, political upheaval—**there is hope available to everyone.** He fully expects us to rise up and claim the rights and privileges of our citizenship under His Kingdom rule.

As God-rule takes over our conduct and our behaviors, we are increasingly transformed into being like Jesus. It is in a state of God ruling in our lives that we encounter His authority. He rules by His authority and acts (carries out His purposes in and through us) by manifesting His power. The **greatest controversy in the Universe** is centered on **who** will have the authority to rule. The **greatest demand of God's Word** is for all mankind to obey Him.

We have been transferred from the domain of darkness into the Kingdom of the Son of His love (Colossians 1:3).

It is the domain (authority) given to us by God that authorizes us to act, thus achieving the result He designates. It is His delegated authority to rule or govern in life. God helps us when we cannot walk, and He helps us when we struggle to walk, but He cannot help us if we do not walk. The point is—let nothing interfere with your walk in Christ.

Circumstances, spiritual status, lack of prayers, or any other such things do not diminish His Kingdom Rule. Prayer is putting our lives into total conformity with God's desires—making ourselves available to Him. Just speak God's Word, His authority, into any situation and watch it perform His purpose.

"So will the words that come out of My mouth not come back empty-handed. They'll do the work I sent them to do, they'll complete the assignment I gave them" (Isaiah 55:11 MSG).

Living the **Fourth Dimension** is about living a God-ruled, God-assigned, God-designed life. **Since you have a choice, why don't you live your highest potential life?** As you make yourself available to Him in total surrender, you will begin to live your unlived life and discover the uniqueness and importance of your Kingdom life.

Keys to Activate Your Kingdom Destiny

Chapter 1

🗝 Understand the difference between your unlived and lived life.

🗝 The Kingdom is the world of *being*, as opposed to our world of *doing*.

🗝 Life is preparing you for your eternity.

🗝 Become the God-designed, God-assigned person you were created to be.

🗝 Your most crucial ability is your availability.

🗝 Challenges should never limit you. You should limit your challenges.

🗝 You and I are more than forgiven—we are destined for the Kingdom.

🗝 Broken focus is one of mankind's greatest curses.

🗝 Victory is defined by Jesus living His life through me.

🗝 In the Kingdom, you fly, you run, you walk.

🗝 We are chosen, changed, and charged by the Kingdom.

Chapter 2

The Kingdom:
It Matters to You

**"The saddest words of tongue or pen
are the words—what might have been."**

AS you look back over your life, what would you change and improve upon? What would you do differently if you had to do it over again? All too often, we are so caught up in our daily world that we pay little attention to the unlived dreams, hopes, and aspirations that have been buried deep within us. No one wants to miss their life. Your time on Earth is fleeting—don't waste it living someone else's life! God created us for the abundant life, the above and beyond life, and He has committed Himself to granting us all that is necessary to achieve that life. It is called the Kingdom Life.

How can anyone deny that man is the apex of God's Creation—more significant than the Universe itself? God has given him laws to rule life and live to the highest level of that life. Some may say *I don't believe in His Kingdom;* however, all scientists agree that the Universe operates by laws. Man is greater than the Universe. God made man a little lower than Himself.

*"Yet You have made him but a little lower than God...,
and You have crowned him with glory and honor"* (Psalm 8:5
AMPC).

Since that is His Truth, you would have to believe He would create laws to govern man, which could cause him to live his **highest life**. Without those laws, man is left to govern his own behavior, which, as we all know, can bring chaos and destruction. Left to himself, man can become a wrecking ball. With God's laws, man is made capable of reaching his highest destiny and living his **God-assigned purpose**. You must submit to these laws. You must "deal" with them. If you fight them, it will have a negative effect on you. If you defy the "Law of Winter" in your swimsuit, it can kill you.

Science can only discover the laws of the Universe; it cannot create them. And without an experience with God—a oneness with Him—man will never grasp the positive power available to him through those laws. If we don't have a oneness relationship with the God Who created those laws, then we can't understand the value and the power of those laws and how they work in our daily lives. All of His Kingdom laws are given to increase and fulfill us. To defy them is to bring a huge limitation, even chaos, into our lives, which is the negative effect of disobedience.

You might defy the **Law of Gravity**, but you could give up your life to do so. In the Universe, there is no such thing as cold—only the absence of heat. **There is no such thing as darkness—only the absence of light.** If you have heat, you will not have cold. **If you have light, you will not have darkness.** These are examples of the thoroughness by which He put the Universe together. His laws are not for our limitations or our destruction, but they are intended for our benefit. They are given to make our lives the highest it can be.

God gave us an entire chapter in Psalm 119 (MSG) with all 176 verses speaking of His laws. He wants to show you the importance of these laws to His Kingdom.

- *Verse 5: "Oh, that my ways were directed and established to observe Your statutes [hearing, receiving, loving, and obeying them]!"*
- *Verse 12: "... teach me Your statutes."*
- *Verse 18: "Open my eyes, that I may behold wondrous things out of Your law."*

All of His laws affect us here on Earth as subjects of His Kingdom, becoming who we will be eternally. Literally, they prepare us for our eternal lives.

"God has placed eternity in our hearts" (Ecclesiastes 3:11).

God placed eternity in our hearts, bringing our sense of wonder. It's beyond our hopes and dreams; eternity is an unknown, unrevealed future. Some aspects are "here and now" (earthly) and "there and then" (heavenly).

How do I become who I really am?
Am I just what happened to me—my choices and decisions?
What if that's not who I truly am?
How do I come to the Truth of my God-assigned identity?
What's beyond this life?

Only by an understanding of the Kingdom will we be able to answer those questions.

Life is a process. Besides the realm of spirit, soul, body into which all of us are born, there is a **Fourth Dimension** of living that makes sense of our spirit, soul, body being. Actually, it may be the only thing that makes sense of us. The wisdom of the ages reveals principles of this life and laws by which we activate this dimension into our living. It is a simplified process of those laws and how to apply them to everyday life. Just saying the **force is with us** does not give us the true meaning of the concept of another dimension of life. In every age and culture, some wise people understand that **we are always more than we have become**, and we may not be **who** we have become. Period.

That search has led mankind down dead-end streets into philosophy, psychology, and metaphysical ideologies that offer no real meaning to life. Those things hold value and reveal much about you; however, they cannot fix you, heal you, or make you into your true self. The vast majority of scientists today believe some force in the Universe caused creation. The Universe has too much order to ignore a common source. Scientists often refer to **unexplainable concepts** of the Universe as **gaps**. Some things just can't be explained scientifically. But that does not diminish the sovereign God Who rules over all. There are just too many repeating patterns and exact mathematical descriptions to ignore the God of the Universe.

God promises, *"While the Earth remains, seedtime and harvest, cold and heat, summer and winter, and day and night, shall not cease" (Genesis 8:22 AMPC).*

"You make darkness, and it is night when all the beasts of the forest creep about" (Psalm 104:20 ESV).

"You cause the grass to grow for the livestock, and plants for man to cultivate, that he may bring forth food from the Earth" (Psalm 104:14 ESV).

"He sends out His command to the Earth; His Word runs swiftly. He gives snow like wool; He scatters hoarfrost like ashes. He hurls down His crystals of ice like crumbs; who can stand before His cold? He sends out His Word, and melts them; He makes His wind blow and the waters flow" (Psalm 147:15-18 ESV).

Some believe life exists on other planets but offer no evidence of that ideology. It's a belief system denying the existence and plan of God Himself. The patterns scientists observe are the laws of God's commitments and His actions. Scientists describe the laws in God's Word ordering the world as so-called natural laws. What they imperfectly observe describes the true laws of God that govern the Universe.

The work of science constantly depends on no deviations in the laws of God that run the Universe. What scientists see is the result of those laws in action, but they don't attribute this to the work of God. Without the laws, there would ultimately be nothing to study. Scientists depend on finding these new laws and exploring the unknowns. Without these, they would have no purpose in their research. They are undoubtedly observing the Kingdom in action without even admitting it exists. The Universe is not the apex of God's Creation—man is. The **Kingdom perspective** is the only thing that makes sense of the human experience—it has a **now-and-then** effect. Every person is born to live with a **Kingdom perspective**. We come from a world of chaos (disorder) into a world of cosmos (order) and experience His Kingdom's power and energy. Once you enter His Kingdom, you decide how close you live to the King.

His Kingdom is **energy** manifested as **power**. Since life is energy, thermodynamics is the study of life. The **Laws of Thermodynamics** define how energy works for us. All matter works toward greater disorder, not greater order. Any system left to itself will, over time, deteriorate unless an outside force is exerted upon that system, thereby regaining some form of order. This is called **entropy—the measure of disorder** in a system.

One act of unbelief and disobedience by Adam began the process of **spiritual entropy** (the measure of disorder in the Earth—sin), which now affects the entire Universe.

"All creation longs for freedom from its slavery to decay and to experience with us the wonderful freedom coming to God's children. To this day we are aware of the universal agony and groaning of creation, as if it were in the contractions of labor for childbirth" (Romans 8:21-22 TPT).

Our world is now moving more and more towards greater disorder and chaos. Left to itself, nothing would stop the process. But God sent His Son, Who introduced His Kingdom—a supernatural force outside Earth's system—to bring about order. He released the laws of the Kingdom in order to bring about an interruption of the deterioration of sin and chaos in our world. The **enemy** wants nothing more than to **devour. God searches to empower.** Therefore, Kingdom Life matters to you and me.

When you move out in faith, God always shows up. **Divine Kingdom opportunities** come when we get up and act. It is a requirement that we are not observers of life but active participants. Live **intentionally on purpose.**

"Be well balanced and always alert, because your enemy, the devil, roams around incessantly, like a roaring lion looking for its prey to devour" (1 Peter 5:8 TPT).

"GOD is always on the alert, constantly on the lookout for people who are totally committed to Him..." (2 Chronicles 16:9 MSG).

You are largely an unexplored life with a creation assignment to develop yourself and produce a harvest beyond your capacity. You will only experience this by living the Kingdom life (which is **Living the Fourth Dimension**).

Spiritual entropy occurs in 1 Samuel 14 through the adventure of Jonathan and his armor bearer. Jonathan greatly expected God to advance His Kingdom based on a prophetic Word given to his father, King Saul. During the time of war with the Philistines, the Israelites realized they were way outnumbered and ran for cover, hiding in caves, pits, ravines, cisterns—wherever. Only Saul and his son Jonathan had a sword and spear for battle.

People who live the Kingdom life understand that they can activate **Kingdom power** and bring **Kingdom victory in any situation**. Jonathan's father, Saul, was drinking pomegranate juice while Jonathan was activating the Kingdom. Some people watch things happen; **Kingdom people make things happen**. Jonathan moved out to seize a divine opportunity. His father played it safe, living in a comfort zone. The Kingdom demands you live intentionally on purpose. Ordinary people throughout history have stepped up in moments of crisis and activated God's Kingdom power to bring about the miraculous.

The Philistines yelled out to him and his armor bearer to come up to where they were. Jonathan knew God had given the Philistines into their hands. He and his armor-bearer killed 20 Philistines and caused a terrific upheaval in their camp, with God shaking the ground underneath them, creating panic (1 Samuel 14:12-16).

That day, God saved Israel and brought order into a chaotic condition—spiritual entropy. A powerful outside force was exerted upon the enemy. Order was restored.

Jesus Christ was the answer to the spiritual entropy in the world. He was God's special, outside force introduced into our chaotic world to bring spiritual order. The manifestation of God's Kingdom on Earth is available to anyone who dares to become Kingdom-minded and seek first His Kingdom and His righteousness.

The forceful entry of Jesus Christ into the Earth was the interruption that began to reverse the deterioration brought about by sin. Just as God originally brought order into the Creation of

Earth in Genesis 1 by saying, *"Light be,"* Jesus accomplished the same thing with His conquering of sin, death, Hell, and the grave.

"In Him was Life, life that made sense of human existence"
(John 1:4 original translation).

Kingdom life demands that you live from your spirit, not just soul and body. We are **Kingdom, spirit-beings**. To live a natural (body and soul) life is only a part of your life. There are **untapped spiritual resources** available to you that will **enlarge your capacity for God**. Those can only be experienced as you pursue a Kingdom life.

When you live by a Kingdom ideology, it's like you are on spiritual steroids. You develop spiritual muscle, stamina, energy, and drive, which propel you to adventures beyond your human capabilities. Mankind was created by God with a spirit of adventure, and until you venture through your Kingdom capacity, you will never know who He created you to be.

"Never doubt God's mighty power to work in you and accomplish all this. He will achieve infinitely more than your greatest request, your most unbelievable dream, and exceed your wildest imagination! He will outdo them all, for His miraculous power constantly energizes you" (Ephesians 3:20 TPT).

The basic demand of His Kingdom is for man to receive it and yield to its control. This is *God's uncreated life* flowing through and empowering our *created life*. God flows His Kingdom life (Divinity) into our human life for a Kingdom purpose.

Without divine alignment, there is no spiritual assignment.

The laws of the Kingdom are designed to bring us into **divine alignment**, which results in **oneness with God**. So it's not a matter of behavior; it's a matter of becoming one with God and acting out His Kingdom mandate in everyday life. These laws are given to us to "become," and then they govern our conduct and behavior, which is the "doing."

When we receive and become dominated by the force and power of His Kingdom, a new dimension of living opens up to us with **limitless possibilities.** His life flows through us as we minister the life of Jesus to those around us who have been wounded, hurt, and beaten down by life.

Living with a **Kingdom perspective** while on Earth causes us to move beyond a spirit-soul-body experience into a **Fourth Dimension Life**. His Kingdom empowers us to move beyond our human experience into a spiritual one. **We are spirit-beings having a human experience.**

From the beginning, He gave us a Kingdom perspective by determining the length of a day. We never live on a yesterday, and we never live on a tomorrow. We only live on a today. The fact that each day ends at midnight gives us a Kingdom perspective on the past. You only get enough sleep in one night to live one day—one night of rest is not enough for three days of living. When we let each day die at midnight, we let the baggage of the past die, and we are given a fresh start for each new day. **Everything about living the Kingdom life is a vast improvement over the spirit-soul-body life.** The Kingdom perspective is always about transformation. Life often comes to deform us, while the Kingdom always comes to transform us. **Kingdom living offers a hope, a promise, and a purpose beyond our wildest imaginations.**

Someone has observed that life is like a dollar bill. You can spend it any way you want to, but you can spend it only once. There are only three ways to spend money: waste it, exchange it for necessities, or invest it. The same is true with life.

Today, whoever you are, wherever you are, you have the opportunity to make the rest of your life the best of your life. If you, beginning today, would consciously, continuously, and consistently **put the Kingdom first, it would absolutely transform your life.** It requires an active pursuit and a willingness to go after the manifestation of His Kingdom through you. That will require Jesus becoming preeminent in your daily life.

All human beings are seekers. We need something to live for, something which gives meaning to our existence, something on which to set our minds and our hearts. Greek philosophers called it **the supreme good** to which we dedicate our lives. Today, we call it **ambition**—a strong desire to achieve success. Ambition concerns our goals in life and our incentives for pursuing them. Ambition can either be self-centered or God-centered. We must be truly ambitious for Jesus to be recognized and honored as our King.

Jesus commands us to be obsessed with His Kingdom—His rule and His reign. **We are to seek the glory of the King.**

> *"...whatever you may do, do all for the honor and glory of God"* (1 Corinthians 10:31 AMPC).

We are to seek the guidance of the King.

> *Lord, what do You expect of me today?*

We are to seek the government of the King. The greatest liberty in the world is to be controlled by Jesus. Only when we make our needs secondary to our relationship with God can we fully devote our energies to seeking His Kingdom. Kingdom-minded people must get their eyes off the circumstances of this world. God's Kingdom can never be diminished by circumstances.

In His Kingdom, there is **absolute abundance**. You and I can have **total favor** with the Ruler of that abundance. As His disciples, we have been permitted to know **the secrets of His Kingdom**.

When God is more real to you than your physical resources, you will never lack.

In His Kingdom, you decree His abundance rather than beg for your needs to be met.

He turns our **successes** into **significance**.
He **graces** us with **His favor**.
He **chooses** us.
He **protects** us.
He **guards** us.
He **assigns angels** to us.

God's Kingdom is Jesus Christ ruling over His people in total blessing and total demand.

To *"seek first His Kingdom"* is to desire, as of first importance, the spread of the reign of Jesus Christ. We must evangelize since the Kingdom grows only as the Gospel of the Kingdom is preached, heard, believed, and obeyed. When we live His Kingdom principles, the heathen, the lost, and the unchurched will see His blessing and favor on our lives and desire to know why. "All these things will be added unto us": life, food, drink, clothing, daily sustenance, gas, money, health, protection, etc.

"No good thing will He withhold from them
that walk uprightly" (Psalm 84:11).

When He sits upon the throne of our hearts, His **Kingdom provision** is **released** within us.

The major passion, theme of Jesus' teaching and ministry was and is the Kingdom. Jesus was passionate about it. In the Gospels,

He spoke of it more than 100 times.

> *"...I must preach the Good News (the Gospel) of the Kingdom of God to the other cities [and towns] also, for I was sent for this [purpose]" (Luke 4:43 AMPC).*

It is perhaps the greatest question one may ask—What is Kingdom life? Life, as Jesus saw it, was not a transient physical condition. He saw us as spirit-beings having a physical experience. For Him, to live was to be in a right relationship with God, to be filled with a sense of His Spirit, love and holiness, or wholeness. This sense of God would dominate every act, thought, and word of man.

God would be his loving King as man would joyfully take his place in the Kingdom and join with others who share the same passion and enthusiasm for it. Through them, this Kingdom would become visible as a culture, a society. Before we pray, **Your Kingdom come**, we must be willing to pray, **my kingdom go**.

God must occupy the highest place in our prayers and indeed in our whole lives. The **Kingdom of God** means **the reign of God**. We must see ourselves as **Kingdom citizens**. Kingdom citizens desire to see the Kingdom of God in every nook and cranny of the Earth.

We must pray for three things:

First, for the final and ultimate **establishment of God's Kingdom**.

> *"...The dominion (kingdom, sovereignty, rule) of the world has now come into the possession and become the Kingdom of our Lord and of His Christ, and He shall reign forever and ever!" (Revelation 11:15 AMPC).*

Second, we desire to **conform to His will** in this world. We surrender ourselves to God so He may do with us as He pleases. *"Your Kingdom come"* into my life—use me for your Kingdom purpose.

Third, it is a **prayer that God's rule will come to others** as He works His convicting power through us—in our families, jobs, businesses, neighborhoods, cities, and nations. This big prayer depends on a big God, and when truly prayed, it creates a big life. Our chief goal as believers is to *"seek first of all His Kingdom and His righteousness..." (Matthew 6:33).*

Since Adam's sin, God has been working out a plan and purpose in which He is gathering a people to Himself and over which He intends to exercise His rule. He enters into a covenant with His people with the precise agenda that they may be His people, and He will be their God. God intends to overthrow all of Satan's works. Praying "**Your Kingdom come**" is so that the kingdom of Satan may be destroyed**.**

> *"...The reason the Son of God was made manifest (visible) was to undo (destroy, loosen, and dissolve) the works the devil [has done]" (1 John 3:8 AMPC).*

The decisive battle has been won at the Cross. Satan refuses to accept his defeat and continues to fight against God's Kingdom—His children. Everywhere, he is working with his schemes and his methods, and he's plotting against God's Kingdom (Ephesians 6:11). You and I are to live as covenant people and demonstrate the power of His Kingdom against every attack of the enemy.

Every time we rise in the power of His Name—Jehovah—and in the power of His Son's Name—Jesus—and in the power of His Holy Spirit, we defeat him and advance God's Kingdom. If I dare to pray— "***Your Kingdom Come on Earth as it is in Heaven***," in my life, in my world, I must be totally committed to Him.

Your best, highest, most productive, most powerful, most influential, most victorious life is your **covenant Kingdom** life—**Living the Fourth Dimension.** Live it, and the results will be powerful beyond belief, but it requires you to surrender, to be surrendered, and continuously surrender.

The **surrendered life** is a life of freedom, peace, fulfillment, and joy. Whatever the circumstances of your birth, they pale in comparison to the opportunity to create your life. The full and complete surrender to Him matters most in His Kingdom. Surrender requires three powerful Kingdom laws:

The Law of Separation
The Law of Dedication
The Law of Consecration

Separation is the pathway to achieving greatness. Abraham separated from his family and friends in order to follow God and become a great nation for Him. David separated himself from King Saul, his family, and his palace residence to live in a cave with a group of malcontents. Moses was separated from his heritage, his family. Jesus was separated from His Father, from Heaven. Paul gives us a powerful command of separation in 2 Corinthians:

> *"So, come out from among [unbelievers], and separate (sever) yourselves from them, says the Lord, and touch not [any] unclean thing; then I will receive you kindly and treat you with favor" (verse 6:17 AMPC).*

If, in fact, you are a unique person—and you are,
and you are created by a divine God—and you are,
and you are made in His likeness and image—and you are,
and your life is a designed plan and purpose—and it is,
then your only choice to live who you really are,
is a complete surrender to His will.

One cannot partially surrender—**surrender is full and complete,** or it is not surrender. (Similar to the idea that you can't be almost pregnant!) Surrendering to Him changes everything. Surrendering is not an act—it is a lifelong process.

God chose us in Him before the world was created (Ephesians 1:4).

By living a Kingdom life, we live in the world, but we are not of it. Literally, the world is never supposed to be in us. After placing us in the world, He called us to live a separate life—to be in the world but not of the world. When we receive Christ as Lord and Savior, He separates us from our sins. We are then responsible for separating ourselves from the world in order to live in the **Fourth Dimension** while we are here on Earth.

Jesus prayed, *"I do not ask that You will take them out of the world, but that You will keep and protect them from the evil one. They are not of the world (worldly, belonging to the world), [just] as I am not of the world. Sanctify them [purify, consecrate, separate them for Yourself, make them holy] by the Truth; Your Word is Truth" (John 17:15-17 AMPC).*

To be forgiven of our sins is only the first step in becoming who God designed us to be. We then must be taught by the Holy Spirit the deeper life of dedication. We **present our bodies**, our bodily members, and our faculties as instruments of righteousness unto God.

Dedication means **to press in**. It is the idea of participation, of aggressively pressing into God. It has a sense of **renewal**. We press into God, giving ourselves totally to Him.

Consecration means **to devote, to set apart, to fill the hand**.

Consecration fills the hand of God with my surrendered life. God then fills my hand, my works, with the tools and means necessary to accomplish His purposes. I become a tool in God's hand, and God puts tools in my hand. The driving power behind my life of separation, dedication, and consecration is the great love He poured out into me. His mighty love, demonstrated in His death on the Cross, becomes my life's moving, motivating energy.

> *"So here's what I want you to do, God helping you: Take your everyday, ordinary life – your sleeping, eating, going-to-work, and walking-around life – and place it before God as an offering. Embracing what God does for you is the best thing you can do for Him. Don't become so well-adjusted to your culture that you fit into it without even thinking. Instead, fix your attention on God. You'll be changed from the inside out. Readily recognize what He wants from you, and quickly respond to it. Unlike the culture around you, always dragging you down to its level of immaturity, God brings the best out of you, develops well-formed maturity in you"* (Romans 12:1-2 MSG).

We become His bond slaves on the day we offer our lives to Him. He purchases us, redeems us, places us as sons, and possesses us for the glory of His Kingdom. He legally owns us, and out of love for Him, we consecrate and put our lives in His hands.

> *"For the love of Christ constraineth us..."*
> *(2 Corinthians 5:14 KJV).*

Constrained means being **tightly held** or surrounded so one cannot escape.

Love is the basis of consecration. Here again, we see the **360-God**. Consecration brings an awareness of His **continual Presence**. Once we fill God's hands with our lives, He fills them with the **treasures of His Kingdom**.

Only when He possesses me can I experience His Presence. His

Presence brings peace, comfort, healing, and protection. I consider my whole life as belonging exclusively to Him.

I love the hymn "I Surrender All."

> All to Jesus I surrender
> All to Him I freely give
> I will ever love and trust Him
> In His presence daily live
> I surrender all
> I surrender all
> All to Thee
> My blessed Savior
> I surrender all

("I Surrender All" by Judson W. Van DeVenter)

Daily, you and I face the decision of how we will spend our lives. There are only two choices:

The flesh-dominated life or the spirit-dominated life.

Each of those choices is an actual law: The **Law of the Spirit of Life** in Christ Jesus or the **Law of Sin and Death** (Romans 8:2). This also comes from the two trees in the Garden: the Tree of Life and the Tree of the Knowledge of Good and Evil. Every day, we choose to live out our lives from one of these trees—a **Christ-centered life** or a **flesh-centered life**.

The issue we face daily is **who or what controls us**. When God is in control of my life, I am never out of control. What I believe determines who I serve. Who I serve determines how I live. How I live determines my destiny.

Only by the Law of the Spirit of Life in Christ Jesus can one live their true **God-assigned life**. God does not beat around the bush regarding His desire for us.

"For in Him we live and move and have our being..."
(Acts 17:28 AMPC).

Two dominant words in Romans 12:1—**living and sacrifice**—appear mutually contradictory. **Living** means to be **full of vigor and overflowing with strength.** **Sacrifice** implies **death and being laid upon an altar waiting to be consumed.** However, there is an underlying harmony in which these two ideas unite. **Sacrifice is not an end but a means.**

In ancient times, the priest would lay the body of a slain animal on an altar to be consumed by holy fire. You and I are to lay our living bodies upon the altar of consecration, *there* to be consumed with the fire of His Spirit. We are then **filled with a divine passion, fired with enthusiasm** for service that will see no task too hard to endure and no cross too heavy to bear. But, it's only when we give to Him our bodies—the instrument and organ of our lives. The act of separation, dedication, and consecration is very challenging, to say the least. It requires a great deal of effort, consistency, and perseverance.

This bumper sticker caught my attention as I pulled up behind a car at the traffic light:

Where the h_ _ _ is Easy Street?
(As you notice, I blatantly never use 4-letter words.)

Obviously, the driver had been struggling with life's demands and was looking for a better, easier life. So, I thought, even if there was an Easy Street, would it actually be the best place to live? No challenges, no lack, no enemies, no struggles, no worries, no fears—just easy living—boring living.

Then, I read about the Bristlecone pine tree, which grows in the Western mountain regions up to two miles above sea level and has lived for thousands of years. With only a thin layer of bark on

THE KINGDOM: IT MATTERS TO YOU

their trunks, they survive in rocky areas with poor soil and slight precipitation. It seems almost incredible they should have lived so long or even at all.

The **environmental adversities contribute to their longevity**. Cells produced due to these perverse conditions are densely arranged, and many resin canals are formed within the plant. Wood that is so structured continues to live for an extremely long period. Bristlecone pines in more pleasant climates grow faster but die earlier and decay. The harshness of their surroundings is vital in making them strong and sturdy.

While living as Kingdom citizens on Earth, it seems we never experience Easy Street. Like Bristlecone pines, we grow strong and sturdy as we graciously accept the challenges God permits into our lives. If we refuse to humble ourselves under the mighty hand of God, He will humble us. **Humility** means **to bring to the ground and to make level**. It is putting others' needs and desires ahead of our own.

God allows things into our lives to reveal that we are insufficient without His sufficiency. **Self-reliance** is pride—**God-reliance** is humility. Humility is an attitude toward God that gives Him credit for who we have become and what we can do.

"Do you want to stand out? Then step down. Be a servant. If you puff yourself up, you'll get the wind knocked out of you. But if you are content to simply be yourself, your life will count for plenty" (Matthew 23:11-12 MSG).

"Casting the whole of your care [all your anxieties, all your worries, all your concerns, once and for all] on Him, for He cares for you affectionately and cares about you watchfully" (1 Peter 5:7 AMPC).

We humble ourselves by *"casting all of our cares upon Him"*

(Psalm 55:22). **Cares** means **to divide or be drawn in different directions.** It is the picture of someone or something being pulled apart. This refers to the whole of your life—everything about you. Surrender up to Him your whole being—spirit, soul, body. Holiness (or wholeness) is the foundational attribute of God. All the other attributes come out of this. **God's holiness** means He is **whole in Himself**. His ultimate desire for you and me is to become whole like He is.

His holiness means He **cares** for you—a totally different word here. Cares means **to be interested in and show continuous watchful care and affection or concern. God is our caretaker—** He cares for us. We are His personal concern.

> *"Be well balanced (temperate, sober of mind), be vigilant and cautious at all times; for that enemy of yours, the devil, roams around like a lion roaring [in fierce hunger], seeking someone to seize upon and devour" (1 Peter 5:8 AMPC).*

He tells us to be **sober-minded**, which is more than not being physically intoxicated; it refers to being free of every form of mental and spiritual intoxication. We live in a culture intoxicated with every form of sexual lust and perversion, sin, and unbelief. The minds and spirits of people are being numbed, lulled to sleep by cultural persuasion to compromise God's Word concerning these permissive attitudes.

As Kingdom citizens **Living the Fourth Dimension**, we are to be **self-controlled, well-balanced**, and **clear-headed**; be cool, calm, collected, steady, even-handed, and alert.

The **sober people** don't live on the surface, a shallow life where culture thrives. Instead, they live deep, hearing from the reservoir of God's Word and wisdom in the depth of their spirits.

Living the Fourth Dimension causes us to arise, be vigilant, watchful, alert, cautious, and fully awake.

"Be alert and on your guard; stand firm in your faith (your conviction respecting man's relationship to God and divine things, keeping the trust and holy fervor born of faith and a part of it). Act like men and be courageous; grow in strength!" (1 Corinthians 16:13).

We are to resist Satan—oppose his attempts to weaken our resolve—and stand firm—stand like a rock with a deep underground foundation.

As you humble yourself, casting your life on Jesus, continuing to be sober and alert, maintaining your convictions, and standing firm like a rock, God will do five things for you.

1. *"He will **perfect** us"* (1 Peter 5:10). Knowing we will be battle-scarred, often wearied, and sometimes broken, He will restore us. The word focuses on a medical and emotional context of health and well-being. It describes "the setting of a bone which has been broken and is positioned and splinted for healing." It is the gentle replacement of a dislocated limb back into its socket.

2. When we are **out of joint**, He **restores us to proper functioning**. God makes us "whole" so that our lives are in working order again.

3. He will **confirm us—make us firm and stable**, as an inward work of His Holy Spirit, causing us to stand erect, no longer bent over from the cares of life.

4. He will **strengthen—increase our capabilities**, fill us with strength, and equip us to handle the demands of life.

5. He will **establish** us. Ground us securely, and He will settle us in His Word. His purpose in these actions is to perfect us in His righteousness.

Paul tells us that the Kingdom is righteousness, with peace and joy in the Holy Spirit.

"So whoever cleanses himself [from what is ignoble and unclean, who separates himself from contact with contaminating and corrupting influences] will [then himself] be a vessel set apart and useful for honorable and noble purposes, consecrated and profitable to the Master, fit and ready for any good work. Shun youthful lusts and flee from them, and aim at and pursue righteousness (all that is virtuous and good, right living, conformity to the will of God in thought, word, and deed); [and aim at and pursue] faith, love, [and] peace (harmony and concord with others) in fellowship with all [Christians], who call upon the Lord out of a pure heart" (2 Timothy 2:21-22 AMPC).

The **ruling principle** that God has sown into the Universe is called the **Law of Righteousness.** God has seeded the Universe with that law. According to the writer of Proverbs, righteousness provides the following:

**It is an identity-revealing power that qualifies us
to become who God says we are.
It is living inside of God's divine order.
It delivers from death.**

"When Judgment Day comes, all the wealth of the world won't help you one bit. So you'd better be rich in righteousness, for that's the only thing that can save you in death"

(Proverbs 11:4 TPT).

—It gives life.

"Abundant life is discovered by walking in righteousness..." (Proverbs 12:28 TPT).

—It exalts a nation.

"A nation is exalted by the righteousness of its people... (Proverbs 14:34 TPT).

—It rewards.

"...to sow seeds of righteousness will bring a true and lasting reward" (Proverbs 11:18 TPT).

—It brings peace.

According to Isaiah 32:16, the end result of righteousness will be peace (internal and external), along with quietness and confident trust forever.

Your welfare, your community's welfare, the nation's welfare, and the world's welfare depend on living in righteousness. This message of **righteousness** (used over 900 times in the Bible) will bring **wholeness, health, discipline, balance,** and **freedom** as we live within His design, His standard for the exemplary life. His world (which includes the Earth; the Earth is the Lord's) is designed to be enjoyed within His stated boundaries—**the Kingdom matters** to the **spiritual order of our world.**

This does not constrict our freedom—it expands it and floods our lives with His grace and mercy. By this grace and mercy, we are equipped to live an **enlarged life.** Grace is receiving that which we do not deserve and cannot earn. Mercy is not receiving what we deserve and earned by unrighteous living.

Righteousness is a gift from God to each of His children, but you must choose and pursue it in your daily life.

One question you answer daily on your life journey is:

Am I bigger than, greater than, the challenges I face?

Our challenges become powerful seeds of success, blossoming into a life of significance. Our significance transcends the occasional seasons of resistance and brings us to serenity.

In every nation, culture, and society, the single most important industry engaged in is the building of people.

God's method for building people is righteousness.

"The [uncompromisingly] righteous shall flourish like the palm tree [be long-lived, stately, upright, useful, and fruitful]; they shall grow like a cedar in Lebanon [majestic, stable, durable, and incorruptible]. Planted in the house of the Lord, they shall flourish in the courts of our God. [Growing in grace] they shall still bring forth fruit in old age; they shall be full of sap [of spiritual vitality] and [rich in the] verdure [of trust, love, and contentment]. [They are living memorials] to show that the Lord is upright and faithful to His promises; He is my Rock, and there is no unrighteousness in Him" (Psalm 92:12-15 AMPC).

The imagery is one of an **ageless, productive life of achievement and fulfillment**.

The palm tree flourishes in the desert as its roots go deep to find water to sustain it. It does not depend on its surroundings or circumstances but on its root system. Righteousness gives us deep roots and the sustaining water of His Spirit. The cedar is an **exogen— it grows outward** from its center to the circumference. Concentric rings indicate its age. It can grow up to 150 feet, and its branches can spread to 300 feet. A righteous man's character is ever-growing, expanding, and being perfected as the world around him observes his growth.

A palm tree is an **endogen** or **inside grower**. The oldest and hardest wood is at the circumference—the newest and softest wood is at the center. It breaks any band put around it. Nothing stops its growth. The older the palm tree, the sweeter the fruit and the more fruit produced—up to 600 pounds in a season. The righteous man grows from his spirit and is not hindered by outside circumstances.

Righteousness brings out our highest and most productive life.

Since the **Law of Righteousness** permeates everything He created, the Universe functions best when operating by this law. Only by understanding the Kingdom, **Living the Fourth Dimension**, can we begin to experience the **ultimate meaning of life**. This is why the Kingdom matters. The more righteous our lives are, the greater the manifestation of His Kingdom's power in and through us.

The artist sows himself into his painting. It is said that talented artists bring their souls into the canvas. They become one with the paintings. When we live the Kingdom life, we are immersing our spirit-soul-body into His life on Earth.

The **degree** to which you **invest yourself** into His Kingdom— gifts, talents, abilities, resources—determines how **fully alive you become**.

That is why the **Kingdom Matters to you** and our world.

Keys to Activate Your Kingdom Destiny

Chapter 2

It matters that...

You were born with a God-assigned purpose and destiny.

You are more than you have become.

You live with a Kingdom perspective.

You have divine Kingdom opportunities.

You have untapped spiritual resources in your Kingdom lifestyle.

You put the Kingdom first.

You have total favor with the Ruler of the Universe.

You consecrate (fill God's hand) your life to God.

You live a spirit-dominated life.

You live the Law of Righteousness.

The Kingdom enlarges your capacity for God.

Through the Kingdom, God is building His people.

The Kingdom brings spiritual order to your life.

In the Kingdom, I am bigger than, greater than, the challenges I face.

The Kingdom:
Manifested

**Miracle of all miracles—human beings may have a
manifestation of the Kingdom that caused creation.**

IMAGINE a way of life far exceeding in Godliness, any conceivable
utopia bordered by the horizons of time and space. The Good News
of His Kingdom is about an ideal society and culture into which all
can be ushered and for which they were created. Empowered by the
Spirit, they engage in a process of living righteously to fill the Earth
with His Kingdom.

His Kingdom message is how we offer our lives—spirit, soul,
body—on the altar of sacrifice so that He can use us to bring glory
to His name. In doing so, you become significantly fulfilled, with
great self-worth and self-esteem. However, sadly, the world offers a
different point of view:

> *"God can get you what you want better than anyone
> else can." "Use God to gain the world, success,
> significance, wealth, health, and blessings galore."*

That, however, is not the message of Jesus, of Paul, of Christianity.

The great Abraham Lincoln wrote about the purposes of our American Government:

"This is essentially a people's contest. It is a struggle for maintaining in the world that form and substance of government whose leading objective is to elevate the condition of men—to lift the artificial weights from their shoulders—to clear the paths of laudable pursuits for all—to afford all an unfettered start and fair chance in the race of life."

What Lincoln is describing actually has a scriptural basis. We are to sojourn here on Earth and live as citizens of a nation, as well as citizens of Heaven. Thus, we have **dual citizenship**. As **citizens of Heaven**, God is our Shepherd, King, and Father. We are sheep, subjects, and children. **Shepherd and sheep**, **King and subjects**, **Father and children** form the rich, intimate relationship that we have with God.

We move from the demands of the law in the Old Testament to a sense of loyalty and obedience to becoming one with God through faith in Jesus Christ. In becoming one with God through faith in Jesus Christ, we see the manifestation of His Kingdom on Earth.

Jesus did these three things pertaining to the Kingdom:

He *proclaimed* the availability of the Kingdom to everyone (*Mark 1:15*).

He *taught* the message of His Kingdom (*Luke 4:43*).

He *manifested* His Kingdom Presence in such a fashion that it could not be explained in a natural way (*Matthew 12:28*).

And wonder of all wonders, He commanded us to do those same things.

You step into His Kingdom, His gift to us, by being born again.

"...Before a person can perceive God's Kingdom realm, they must first experience a new birth" (John 3:3 TPT).

It is much like gravity—you can't walk without gravity, but if you wait for gravity to make you walk, you will never walk. Jesus didn't come just to take up space in your heart and passively sojourn with you on your earthly pilgrimage. His message to us, within us, and through us is one of an **interactive partnership** in Kingdom works.

Unfortunately, the vast majority of Christians today seem to have a passive view of life in the Kingdom. Their thinking is: I am now born again, my name is in the Lamb's Book of Life, and when I die, I am going to Heaven. But the life that Jesus has called us to is a **joint venture** fueled by **His Word and His Holy Spirit** to expand His Kingdom on Earth. **We must release God into the world through deeds, words, and actions.** By doing so, we will rule and reign as kings in life. Our **natural life becomes supernatural** as we move beyond mere human gifts, talents, and abilities.

God actively seeks those who will worship Him in Spirit and in Truth. **Seeking** is the key to understanding how to enter His Kingdom and live as His disciples.

"But seek (aim at and strive after) first of all His Kingdom and His righteousness (His way of doing and being right), and then all these things taken together will be given you besides" (Matthew 6:33 AMPC).

"After this, the Lord Jesus formed thirty-five teams among the other disciples. Each team was two disciples, seventy in all, and He commissioned them to go ahead of Him into every town He was about to visit. He released them with these instructions: 'The harvest is huge. But there are not enough harvesters to

bring it in. As you go, plead with the Owner of the Harvest to send out many more workers into His harvest fields'" (Luke 10:1-2 TPT).

God wants to be needed, desired, hungered for, and pursued. When we seek the Kingdom of God, we intend to allow God to be present in everything we are and do. We allow Him to act, overrule, guide, and help us become who He created us to be. First, however, we must seek, prefer, desire, and inquire of Him with our entire being.

"'When you come looking for Me, you'll find Me. Yes, when you get serious about finding Me and want it more than anything else, I'll make sure you won't be disappointed.' GOD's Decree" (Jeremiah 29:13 MSG).

Your **Kingdom position** is determined by the **forgiveness of sins**. There is no greater action in any society or culture than to experience forgiveness. No sweeter word exists in any language.

Forgiveness is the **promise** of the Father.

It is the **provision** of Jesus.

It is the **proclamation** of His Word.

It is the **power** of the Holy Spirit.

It is the required **practice** of His Kingdom.

Forgiveness is **part** of the declared nature of God.

*"And when you pray, make sure you forgive the faults of others so that your Father in Heaven will also forgive you. **But if you withhold forgiveness from others, your Father withholds forgiveness from you**"* (Matthew 6:14-14 TPT).

We are simply required to ask for it as He is more ready to forgive us of our sins than we are to forsake our sins. **Forgiveness is the most liberating law of God's Kingdom.**

Sin has so marred, scarred, and warped us that merely pardoning us would be grossly insufficient. We need a chance to start over. We must be transformed to have a released spirit, a renewed mind, and a guiltless conscience. His forgiveness restores our relationship with Him. We are reconciled and restored to fellowship by His manifested love. **Love fuels all the activities of the Kingdom**. *"For God so loved...."* The word **forgive** means to send forth or away from one's self. It means to remit (to release from the penalty or guilt of sin).

David experienced God's forgiveness after his sin with Bathsheba.

"What happiness for those whose guilt has been forgiven! What joys when sins are covered over! What relief for those who have confessed their sins and God has cleared their record" (Psalm 32:1-2 TLB).

You are never closer to the grace of Jesus than when you confess your sins to Him.

"He Who covers his transgressions (hides, keep secret) will not prosper (accomplish success), but whoever confesses and forsakes his sins will obtain mercy" (Proverbs 28:13 AMPC).

You are never more like Jesus than forgiving those who have sinned against you. Until you are forgiven, and you forgive, you will never enter your Kingdom covenant. These two freedoms go together. Holding onto grudges, grievances, and resentments chain you to your past.

You block God's covenant blessings from being showered upon your life. **An unforgiving spirit is incredibly detrimental to health—spirit, soul, body.** Bitterness from an offense is one of the most dangerous plagues to a healthy life. It affects your entire being.

To forgive means to release someone **from the wrong** they have done to you. Sometimes, you have to **give up your right to be right**. You give up your right to be offended, retaliate, and get back at them. When you pray, *"Forgive me as I forgive others,"* you are saying, "O God, deal with me as I deal with others." If you pray this prayer while refusing to forgive others who have wronged you, it becomes a self-inflicted curse instead of it bringing God's blessing.

Before your answered prayer comes, before your healing comes, before your deliverance comes, you must forgive others. Before you offer your worship, forgive others.

> *"So if when you are offering your gift at the altar you there remember that your brother has any [grievance] against you, leave your gift at the altar and go. First make peace with your brother, and then come back and present your gift"* (Matthew 5:23-24 AMPC).

At first glance, this verse seems so unfair and unjust. I have no unforgiveness concerning my brother — he is offended by me, yet God puts the responsibility upon me to go to him. Whether my brother receives me is beyond the issue. It is my willingness to be at peace with all men, which God honors. **When someone has an unforgiving spirit, they block the manifestation of the Kingdom of God** through their life, thus preventing them from **Living the Fourth Dimension.**

What God has given to us, He desires to be given to others. His forgiveness is conditional upon our forgiveness of the wrongs done to us. We must also practice forgiving ourselves—something we often struggle with. Scripturally, we have no choice but to emulate God as it relates to forgiving ourselves. Since He has forgiven us in Christ Jesus and our sins are forgotten, we must forgive ourselves. An unforgiving spirit is a terrible burden to bear in this life since we constantly face the temptation to sin on every hand.

What does it mean to sin? In the New Testament, **sin** means you **miss the mark** when you can hit the target. There is a significant difference between the temptation of sin itself and the practice of sin. To be tempted does not mean you have committed a sin.

"Let no one say when he is tempted, I am tempted from God; for God is incapable of being tempted by [what is] evil and He Himself tempts no one. But every person is tempted when he is drawn away, enticed and baited by his own evil desire (lust, passions). Then the evil desire, when it has conceived, gives birth to sin, and sin, when it is fully matured, brings forth death" (James 1:13-15 AMPC).

The Bible is very clear about temptation:

You will be tempted. (James 1:14)

Temptation can bless or curse you: When you are patient under trial and stand up to temptation...you will receive (the victor's) crown of life. (James 1:12)

God always provides a way of escape. (1 Corinthians 10:13)

You can overcome temptation. (Revelation 12:11)

Temptation is a solicitation, a seduction to evil. God tries to help us discover our moral qualities and character. Satan tempts us to delude us, causing us to fall and fail. **Temptation** is not a sin—it is **a call to battle**. Every temptation is an opportunity to draw closer and become more intimate with God.

God permits tests to strengthen us in our walk with Him. Satan tempts us to cause us to stumble. This is the same approach he used when dealing with Jesus in the Wilderness.

"Then Jesus was led (guided) by the [Holy] Spirit into the wilderness (desert) to be tempted (tested and tried) by the devil" (Matthew 4:1 AMPC).

God's purpose in allowing a test of our faith is to refine us, not destroy us. God never promised we would miss the storm—but He has promised we would experience safe harbor. When Jesus taught us to pray—*"And lead us not into temptation"*—He was saying, "Don't allow us to come under the sway of temptation that will overpower us and cause us to sin."

*James 1:13-15 gives us the **source**, the **force**, and the **course** of temptation.*

The **source** of our temptation to sin is within us. Paul warns us we will reap what we sow. While there may be pleasure in sin for a season, the pain comes when you reap what you have sown relative to sin.

"Blessed is that man who is patient under trial and stands up under temptation" (James 1:12).

The conflict educates, strengthens, and establishes you. It causes you to be grounded, settled, approved, and rewarded, but only when you resist the temptation.

We are tempted when we are drawn away (enticed) out of our place of spiritual security and seduced by Satan's bait. The word **enticed** has the meaning to **delude**, **allure**, or **entrap**. In Latin, it means "to stir the fire, to provoke." Our own lust creates temptation. Conquered temptation knits the fibers of our souls into strong muscular cords.

Verse 15—Then the evil desire, when it has conceived, gives birth to sin.

We move from our **emotions** (desire) to our **intellect** (deception) to our **will**.

If this fleshly desire is not dealt with quickly, it germinates in the mind to the point it consumes and deceives our thinking. Lust is fertilized, and sin is birthed when we make provisions to gratify the evil desire.

To **conceive** means **to take, seize, trap, and capture**. Sin is the result of the consummation of the desire inwardly and outwardly.

When sin is fully matured, it brings forth death—spiritual death.

Temptation—

Recognize the **source**.
It comes from our own lusts.

Recognize the **force**.
It dwells in our desires and is powerfully deceptive.

Recognize the **course**.
It leads to death if not aborted.

What God commands us to do, He will enable us to do. He always supplies His power to accomplish His Word.

Our choice to deal with unforgiveness and temptation with a **Kingdom mindset** empowers us as valuable vessels for His Kingdom's sake. When we are seen forgiving others and resisting temptation, a message is sent to the world around us that we are marching to a different drumbeat— **Living the Fourth Dimension**.

The greatest manifestation of His Kingdom in people's lives is the salvation of a soul, accomplished by a mighty act of God's grace. Man's sin presupposes his need for deliverance, which is two-fold: He is delivered from the possession of Satan and delivered into the **possession** of Jesus through the power of His Kingdom. Jesus instructs us to pray and be delivered from the evil one. From Genesis to Revelation, we see two opposing, separate, and distinct Kingdoms: the Kingdom of God and the kingdom of Satan. Each kingdom is competing to exercise authority over mankind.

Satan seeks to enslave and oppress, while **Jesus delivers and grants each of His children free moral agency**. The Kingdom of Darkness deceives and blinds man to the Truth of God's Word, while the **Kingdom of Light illuminates Him**. You and I have the privilege of participating in it.

Jesus delivered us from far more than the power of sin. He rescued us from the authority, the dominion, and the control of darkness. The dimensions of this deliverance are expressed in **resurrection** power, **ascension** power, and **dominion** power.

God, our Father, **provided our deliverance**.
God, the Son, **produced our deliverance**.
God, the Holy Spirit, **empowered our deliverance**.

The same power that worked in Jesus to **resurrect** Him from the dead and caused Him to **ascend** to God's right hand now works in us, causing us to have **dominion**.

"[For it is He (God)] Who rescued and saved us from such a perilous death, and He will still rescue and save us; in and on Him we have set our hope (our joyful and confident expectation) that He will again deliver us [from danger and destruction and draw us to Himself]" (2 Corinthians 1:10 AMPC).

Sometimes, an old piece of furniture glued together separates at a joint as the glue decomposes and loses its cohesive force to hold it together.

John uses the word **undo** to describe this:

"...The reason the Son of God was made manifest (visible) was to undo (destroy, loosen, and dissolve) the works the devil [has done]" (1 John 3:8 AMPC).

By the power of the life of Jesus within us, the works of Satan become unglued and lose their consistency. **Evil** is every kind of **sin**, all dominion that is contrary to God's will. Jesus wants to **emancipate** us and cause the utter extinction of evil in its effect upon us—all human suffering, disease, affliction, and sorrows. Our most potent weapon and defense in the struggle with our own and the world's evil is the earnest prayer of our hearts—*"Deliver us from the evil one!"* Through the experience of battle, we grow and develop, increasing our resistance to the subtle attacks of the enemy. Literally, **Jesus reduced to a zero Satan's ultimate power** over the saints—the power of death.

> *"[God] disarmed the principalities and powers that were ranged against us and made a bold display and public example of them, in triumphing over them in Him and in it [the Cross]"* (Colossians 2:15 AMPC).

These are military terms. Jesus stripped Satan of all his power.

To Satan, He said:

> You were created Lucifer, **Day Star**, but now I am the **Bright** and **Morning Star**.
>
> You were the **anointed cherub**, but now I am the **Anointed One**.
>
> You function as the **tempter**, but now I am a **Guide** and **Comfort** to humanity.
>
> You are a **hinderer**, but now I am a **Helper**.
>
> You are an **adversary**, but now I am their **Ally**.
>
> You function as an **angel of light**, but I am the **Light of the World**.
>
> You are the **accuser of the brethren**, but now I am their **Advocate**.
>
> You are the **prince of this world**, but now I am the **Prince of**

Life, the **King of Kings**, and the **Lord of Lords**.

Jesus came to manifest His Kingdom on Earth to accomplish our total and complete deliverance, to separate us from the evil one.

As we walk out this mighty deliverance each day, our lives are transformed by His manifested power. Our highest life is experienced when we fully and completely surrender our hearts to Him, manifesting His Kingdom power to those around us.

"Unto You, O Lord, do I bring my life" (Psalm 25:1 AMPC).

Your life is a gift from God to you. His greatest gift to you is <u>you</u>.

What you accomplish with your life is your gift back to God. Your life is a treasure—actually, a hidden treasure. Buried within you, God has placed **time**, **talent**, and **treasure**. He designs your life and permits challenges, trials, tests, and temptations to reveal you to you. Life's challenges are meant to expand, enlarge, magnify, and transform you to the degree that you wholly surrender yourself to God.

"My son, give Me your heart and let your eyes observe and delight in My ways" (Proverbs 23:26 AMPC).

First, the Macedonian Christians gave **themselves** to the Lord.

"Nor [was this gift of theirs merely the contribution] that we expected, but first they gave themselves to the Lord and to us [as His agents] by the will of God [entirely disregarding their personal interests, they gave as much as they possibly could, having put themselves at our disposal to be directed by the will of God]" (2 Corinthians 8:5 AMPC).

It is easy to give where the heart is given first. For them, the Lord, His work, and His Kingdom became their passion and purpose.

"For from Him and through Him and to Him are all things.

[For all things originate with Him and come from Him; all things live through Him, and all things center in and tend to consummate and to end in Him.]..." (Romans 11:36 AMPC).

Once you grasp and obey His command of total surrender and step fully into your new Kingdom life, no journey is too difficult, no task too hard, no load too heavy, and no trial too severe. Your **Kingdom mindset becomes your new life walk. Wholeness** of life is possible and is found in hearing and obeying God's Word.

"My son, attend to My words; consent and submit to My sayings. Let them not depart from your sight; keep them in the center of your heart. For they are life to those who find them, healing and health to all their flesh" (Proverbs 4:20-22 AMPC).

When you yield yourself and your heart to the Lord, all other interests and possessions will be under His control—spirit, soul, body. You experience the fullest measure of God in your life when you completely give Him **you**.

God has always wanted only one thing from you—you!

God commands us to protect our hearts. In ancient times, the heart was considered the seat of the will and thought-life. It was in the **heart—the innermost self—**that the personhood of a man or woman was centered. Often it was used as a symbol for the **whole, inner, spiritual** aspect of a **person**.

When God sent the plagues against Egypt, it was Pharaoh's heart that was hardened, meaning his will *(Exodus 9:7).*

So very often, many Christians have a half-hearted approach in their service to God and His Kingdom—the intellect is engaged, but the heart is not activated.

Your **heart** is your whole inner life—your **thought life**, values, choices, passions, and sense of right and wrong. Here is what we are to do with it—

> *"Keep and guard your heart with all vigilance and above all that you guard, for out of it flow the springs of life" (Proverbs 4:23 AMPC).*

We are to **protect, guard, keep, and watch it**. And we are to do that with all diligence. Let nothing enter your heart that would cause you to disobey God's Word. **Springs** refers to a property's boundary lines—the limit of one's property. That is why God demands your heart—yourself. **You determine, by your heart, the limitations of your life.**

As Kingdom citizens living on the Earth, we must continuously be all-in. That means every day, you must realize that God is bringing people across your path to reveal Himself to them through you. In this manner, the Kingdom of God is manifested billions of times daily through those who have become Kingdom citizens. This requires **being sensitive to God's Spirit** as we interact with the people of our lives. Our humanity should never determine the limitations of our lives, but our surrender to the **manifestation of His Kingdom** should.

You are always more than you have become.
Your human life + your Kingdom life = His life on the highest level possible.

Just as Adam and Eve in the Garden met with God in the cool of the day, God wants to manifest His Kingdom life through us daily.

Adam was given the privilege of this relationship in the Garden. Every day, God came to talk with him. His life, existence, and earthly rulership (dominion) depended on this daily meeting with God. Likewise, God never intended for you and me to go, even one day, without being in His Presence. That is the message of *Matthew 6* when we are taught to pray, *"Give us this day our daily bread."*

In Jesus' time, people often buried valuables in a treasure-like box. In an archeological dig, such a box was discovered, and it contained a piece of paper with the words "daily bread," which in Greek refers to a grocery list. Jesus uses the same word to refer to our daily spiritual needs—things that sustain us.

Many believers are spiritually malnourished today. A **weekend service** (feeding) is just **not enough**. Life on Earth often becomes tiresome and monotonous when it is void of the Kingdom concept. Life in the Kingdom (the **Fourth Dimension**) brings a spirit of **adventure**, **excitement**, and **joy**—the fullest life possible.

As the Kingdom is manifested, we proclaim it to the world. Everything about the Kingdom of God being manifested on Earth speaks of life—God's **uncreated life** being poured into your **created life**. Life in the Kingdom is the highest and best adventure afforded to mankind.

Everything you need to live this joyous, fulfilled life is already within you. The treasure stored there is of greater value than all of Earth's treasures. He desires us to create our lives from the treasure He placed within us. You can live the life you create, or you can live the one you allow others or circumstances to create for you. What is within you is far more important than what is around you.

As you exercise your God-given gifts to others, you add value to yourself and others, and you bring glory to God's Kingdom.

"For You did form my inward parts; You did knit me together in my mother's womb" (Psalm 139:13 AMPC).

"Your eyes saw my unformed substance, and in Your book all

the days [of my life] were written before ever they took shape,
when as yet there was none of them" (Psalm 139:16 AMPC).

God gave me life.
God gave me gifts.

God sees and knows me as the work of His hands, empowered by His gifts. He has assigned me a place in life no one else can fill—only He understands and fulfills me. He accomplishes this by choosing a course of action for my specific education by His fatherly love and wisdom.

We have received special gifts and a God-given ability to serve Him and others for His Kingdom's sake. The gifts are to be **accepted**, **explored**, **developed**, and **matured** by the power of the Holy Spirit. When we exercise our spiritual gifts, we are enriched, fellow believers are enhanced, and often, unbelievers are convicted of sin. **Spiritual gifts** are God-given abilities to channel His **love**, **power**, and **miracles** through us **to meet the spiritual needs of others**.

1 Corinthians 12:7 says you are given a gift for the common good.

"As each of you has received a gift, employ it for one another as [befits] good trustees of God's many-sided grace [faithful stewards of the extremely diverse powers and gifts granted to Christians by unmerited favor]" (1 Peter 4:10 AMPC).

Challenges and difficulties often make a demand on your spiritual gifts. They serve as opportunities for you to be increased as you appropriate your gifts. **He strategically places you** where your gift can be most effectively utilized.

As you employ your gift, your confidence grows, you mature, you increase in boldness, your self-esteem rises, you gain respect and recognition, and doors open. Your gift is fully revealed and confirmed as you live your life. God graces us with our gifts. He is always active on behalf of His struggling children.

"A man's gift makes room for him and brings him before great men" (Proverbs 18:16 AMPC).

Either you make room for your gift, or your gift will make room for you. This calls for a total surrender of your gift at the Cross. As you take your gift through the Cross, you release it into His hands. It is then that your gift makes room for you.

By His grace, He comforts us, regulates our circumstances (won't permit more than we can bear), increases our strength, and lifts and encourages our spirits. **Grace is the fruit of His orchard. Grace** comes from a root word meaning **that which gives pleasure and is truly delightful.** With His grace, He **pleasures, delights, and blesses us with beauty, joy, and loving-kindness**. He delights in making us know we are His inheritance.

"You, O God, did send a plentiful rain; You did restore and confirm Your heritage when it languished and was weary" (Psalm 68:9 AMPC).

Confirm means to **be erect (to stand up), to establish, or to prepare**. Literally, to comfort, strengthen, cause to try again, or to lift from discouragement and despair. When we are bowed down with life's burdens, He causes us to stand up. He **rains** on us and **refreshes our spirits**. Then He commands us to *"employ our gift for others and so manage His manifold grace"* (1 Peter 4:10).

The Kingdom of God was manifested from Jesus to us so that we could manifest the Kingdom to others. We do that best when the laws of the Kingdom rule our lives.

"Men must be governed by God, or they will be ruled by tyrants." —William Penn

Concerning humanity, there should be no question as to the mission of Jesus coming to Earth—to allow all of us to be the sons and daughters of God and to be ruled by Him. Only God could be so intelligent as to design a life that would produce **His best** out of **life's worst**. Everything God permits into our lives—good or bad—increases our Kingdom value. He loudly proclaims that man is made in God's image and man can do nothing without Him. It is comforting to know that when He sovereignly controls our lives, they can never be out of control.

God's gift of life to us was always to make us, never to break us.

We question God out of fear—we trust Him out of faith. God is the source of all life. He did not just create us—He sustains us. His desire was for all humanity to be one with Him and obedient to His Word.

"And He made from one man every nation of mankind to live on all the face of the Earth, having determined allotted periods and the boundaries of their dwelling place..." (Acts 17:26 ESV).

His Word establishes His rule concerning man:

All people are created equal in God's image.
All are equally and deeply loved by Him.
All are afflicted and limited by sin.
All are candidates for His redemption.

The doctrine of Christian equality states that all people, regardless of their background, are significant, loved, fallen, and redeemable. His rule determines our individual history.

He made the nations.
He determined the time they would exist.
He drew up the boundaries.

The only way this works is when we submit to **Living the**

Fourth Dimension, which brings about a bond of unity through the manifestation of His Kingdom.

"...He is the ruler over all the nations" (Psalm 22:28 AMPC).

In every battle, election, and situation that rises with power, He has the final say.

Even in those events that seem out of control, God is at work behind the scenes, directing and ruling man's affairs. **You are where you are right now because God has strategically positioned you there**. His goal has always been an intimate, personal relationship. We have the ability and the opportunity to enjoy the absolute fullness of life available to all those who choose to live in the power of the **Fourth Dimension**.

This is a true, meaningful, fulfilling life on the highest level. This life sees every obstacle, every challenge, and every difficulty as an environment in which potential will be released through us.

" ...for in Him we live and move and have our being" (Acts 17:28 NKJV).

In Him—in His rule—we live.

We move, are moved, which deals with our passions, fears, love, anger, and emotional state. It denotes our constant dependence on Him as we process our emotions.

You are either moving with Him or moving without Him. You are moving in His will or moving in your own will. You are doing life His way, or you are doing it your way. Then you have **your being, your existence**—you become who **He designed you** to be.

Inside each one of the 60+ trillion cells in your body is a DNA code that contains every part of your physical existence—your gender, height, the color of your eyes and hair, right or left-handed, etc. Only when you are God-ruled will you live, move, and exist as

He created you to.

We come from God; we answer to God, and we cannot live our Fourth Dimension lives until He rules us by His Word and by His Spirit.

The fact is, you are a secret in your true spiritual being, known only to God. He has designed a **Secret Place** to reveal who you are, why you are, and what you are.

Keys to Activate Your Kingdom Destiny

Chapter 3

 God desires to be manifested in and through my life daily.

 Forgiveness is required to manifest God's Kingdom—of myself and others.

 God manifests His gift of life in and through me.

 He manifests time, talent, and treasure, revealing the purpose of me.

 He manifests His Kingdom life within me so I can live my highest lifestyle.

 He manifests His gifts in me for my acceptance, exploration, and development.

 He manifests His grace to me to pleasure, delight, and bless me.

 He manifests the gift of life to make me—never to break me.

The Kingdom: A Secret Place

The #1 Kingdom rule is—**the Kingdom rules!**

ONE day, as I was riding my bike, I suddenly felt compelled to stop and meditate about God and His Kingdom. I could hear in my spirit: Do you know the #1 rule of the Kingdom? Several answers cropped into my mind. Then I heard His voice say, "The #1 rule of the Kingdom is: The Kingdom rules!" That moment is indelibly imprinted onto my heart, and it caused me to do much research on God's Kingdom. I learned the Kingdom refers to domain or dominion. Our destiny, wealth, purpose, assignment, and reason for being here are to discover and live within the boundaries of His Kingdom, which are based on Kingdom laws. God doesn't run His Kingdom based on emotions. Live by the laws of His Kingdom, and you will live the highest life possible.

In the beginning, there was a Secret Place called the Garden of Eden where Adam and Eve communed with God daily about life. While that possibility is no longer physically available, He has provided for us the **Secret Place of God Most High**, where we may come and **commune with Him** inside our human spirits. It was King David who gave us the beautiful picture of being able to have a conversation with God where He would discuss His Kingdom business on Earth. This also happened in Luke 9 on the Mount of Transfiguration, where Moses and Elijah appeared with Jesus and discussed His Kingdom business on Earth. Life makes sense only to the degree that **we live as Kingdom citizens** during our earthly pilgrimages. The supreme purpose of our lives is the **quest**, the **search**, the **adventure** of entering into His Kingdom.

Jesus commands us to *"seek first His Kingdom and His righteousness" (Matthew 6).*

Righteousness is the foundation of your Kingdom life. Your Kingdom life consists of righteousness, peace, and joy in the Holy Spirit. You discover His Kingdom within you at the core of your being (Luke 17:21). **The church is not just a social organization but a spiritual organism.** It is the agency of His Kingdom—with the primary purpose of bringing people into a right relationship with God. The most powerful, liberating, empowering, equipping truth is not knowing **what I am to do** but **who I am to be.**

People often confuse the church and the Kingdom, but as we have seen, they are two separate entities. Remember, Jesus instituted His Church as a spiritual organism. Through a diligent study of the Scriptures, we come to know our true Kingdom identity.

"He who dwells in the Secret Place of the Most High shall remain stable and fixed under the shadow of the Almighty [Whose power no foe can withstand]. I will say of the Lord, He is my Refuge and my Fortress, my God; on Him I lean and rely, and in Him I [confidently] trust!" (Psalm 91:1-2 AMPC).

The key to being **in the Secret Place** is the word **dwells**. It means one that sits enthroned—to settle down, to inhabit. God wants to abide there with you. Only two can meet there—**your human spirit** and **the Holy Spirit**. When we permanently dwell there, we become

Kingdom subjects—citizens ruled by Him. You and I live in the land of **doing**; however, the **Kingdom is the land of being**.

> *"[After all] the Kingdom of God is not a matter of [getting the] food and drink [one likes], but instead it is righteousness (that state which makes a person acceptable to God) and [heart] peace and joy in the Holy Spirit" (Romans 14:17 AMPC).*

His peace rules there.
He removes the threat out of your yesterday.
He takes the depression out of today.
He casts the fear out of tomorrow.
"Happiness" happens, but His joy abides.

It is the acceptance of His righteousness that brings us into harmony with His will and purpose for our lives. God's intended order and His design for humanity are for each of us to submit to His Kingdom's laws and live daily in obedience to them. To understand God and His salvation, we must grasp what His Kingdom is. Life makes sense to the degree that we live as Kingdom subjects. To the degree to which you live His righteousness, your life aligns with His Kingdom purpose.

Joy is inner gladness based on a spiritual reality. It is Who He is, and it brings a sense of deep-seated well-being. As a Kingdom citizen, joy becomes my strength as I experience His Kingdom rule. Buried within us is that spiritual identity that reveals the purpose of our being. **It is in the Secret Place that you determine who God created you to be.** Included in your identity is a radical obedience to His will and plan for you that causes you to be a conqueror, an overcomer, and a victor.

The one who **abides** in the **Secret Place** of the Most High dwells in an **ascended place of rest**—lifted above the surrounding madness of this fallen world of shadows and darkness.

**In the Secret Place, we experience
His wrap-around Presence—the 360-God.**

He opens the treasures of His Secret Place to whom He chooses, thus giving us greater wisdom and understanding as we face our everyday lives.

From those who live in the Secret Place, He chooses whomsoever He desires to accomplish His purposes and His will. In the Garden, God revealed to Adam and Eve their identity: Adam—of the earth, and Eve—mother of all mankind. Identity was critical to God from **the very beginning**.

Today, command yourself to enter His Secret Place because there you will find all the elements of your **spiritual identity.** Your spiritual DNA is buried in the core of your being and reveals the purpose of your life.

David reveals the beauty of our confidence and stability in Christ in Psalm 16:8:

"Because you are close to Me and always available, my confidence will never be shaken, for I experience Your wrap around Presence every moment" (TPT).

The Lord God Jehovah draws us to the Secret Place to reveal **we are more than we have become**.

"And I will give you the treasure of darkness, and hidden secrets of hidden places, that you may know it is I, the Lord, the God of Israel Who calls you by your name" (Isaiah 45:3 AMPC).

With Him, the **Secret Place is personal and intimate**.

- Is it possible for me to commune with, counsel with, be friends with, and have fellowship with the Living God?

- How is it that a mortal human being can interrelate to the Living God of the Universe?

- How can I—a created being—relate to God—an uncreated being?

- What is the place—the experience—that makes this possible?

The answers to these pertinent questions are only found in surrendering to His will, plan, and purpose for your life. Living communion with a Living God brings His **Presence** into our lives. In that experience, you know the energy, the passion, the power, the boldness, and the confidence of a **God-centered life.**

Imagine the Lord of all Creation offering to co-partner with us in our daily living. He invites us to commune with, counsel with, be friends with, and have fellowship with Him, the Creator of the Universe. There, He instructs, teaches, and counsels us as a friend. He personally tutors us—gives direct commands—equips us with His wisdom, and fills us with His knowledge.

"Every violent thug is despised by the Lord, but every tender lover finds friendship with God and will hear His intimate secrets" (Proverbs 3:32 TPT).

Friend in the Bible is a **covenant** word. Abraham is called the *"friend of God"* in James 2:23.

God spoke to Moses *"face to face as a man speaks to his friend" (Exodus 33:11).* God invites us into His Secret Place for an intimate relationship with Him to reveal His purposes.

"The secret [of the sweet, satisfying companionship] of the Lord have they who fear (revere and worship) Him, and He will show them His covenant and reveal to them its [deep, inner] meaning" (Psalm 25:14 AMPC).

We may translate "secret" in this verse as **counsel** or **council**. **Counsel provides direction** or advice as to a course of action. A **council** is a group of people who **come together to consult**, deliberate, or make decisions. The idea of this word is **perfect union**, **perfect harmony** because of no discord. It also has the connotation of intimacy and relationship. The Hebrew word for **"secret"** indicates **confidential conversation**, speech, or talk. It is a picture of **people sitting on the couch** in a confidential setting.

In the Hebrew picture of this verse, we

> are convinced of His reality,
> know His dealings with us,
> sense His Presence,
> experience His favor, goodness,
> commune with Him on His couch, and
> are filled with His Truth.

Sensing His heart, I realize His thoughts and plans for me. He confides in me my value to His Kingdom on Earth. He reveals to me secret things that my lips should never speak. These are for my edification, which makes it an ever-enlarging place of empowerment, equipping, and education. He leaves nothing out—nothing is ever wasted. Secrets that I would never be able to comprehend are revealed to me here. **The education, the enlightenment of my spirit is the most important educational experience of my life.**

When I know who I am in my human spirit, I know Who He is.

Life in the Secret Place is a safe place where we experience trust. **Protection, security,** and **safety** are words that **define trust for us.** Biblically, it means **to be secure without fear.** Throughout the Bible, we encounter those who constantly lived a life close to God and were greatly favored by Him—being secure without fear. The greatest challenge we face in our journeys is failing to trust God completely in our daily living. **Things that look impossible become Him-possible.**

God knew that life would sometimes become overwhelming, and thus, He provided a Secret Place (the **Fourth Dimension**) for us to abide in continuously.

> *"We all experience times of testing, which is normal for every human being. But God will be faithful to you. He will screen and filter the severity, nature, and timing of every test or trial you face so that you can bear it. And each test is an opportunity to trust Him more, for along with every trial God has provided for you a way of escape that will bring you out of it victoriously"* (1 Corinthians 10:13 TPT).

When the Bible speaks of the Secret Place, it refers to an area of **protection, defense,** and **security.** God surrounds us there because we are sealed, marked as His own. **The Secret Place** is where God reveals His heart as He covers and protects us. As we enter the Secret Place, His knowledge, trust, and thoughts about us mend and restore us. His wisdom guides us through our challenges and difficulties. As we apply what we learn, our spiritual knowledge increases and multiplies.

However, what He says to us is not always to be communicated with our mouths. We learn things that our lips should never speak. The wisdom and knowledge we gain confront worldly wisdom and knowledge and the ugly truths of our sometimes devastating, fearful, disobedient lives. There, I graciously receive His thoughts and plans for me. He confides in me my value to His Kingdom on Earth. I become who He says I am. **Life in the Secret Place is good.**

> *"'For I know the plans and thoughts that I have for you,' says the LORD, 'plans for peace and well-being and not for disaster, to give you a future and a hope'"* (Jeremiah 29:11 AMP).

His goal for our being in His Presence in the Secret Place is **transformation**. The word indicates the action of changing form. We become more of our spiritual selves. This transformation is necessary to bring us into a spiritual thought life where we begin to think the thoughts of God. When we believe in Jesus Christ as our Lord and Savior, we experience salvation. At that moment, we are saved, we are being saved, and we shall be saved. You are not all that you are created to be at that moment, but the **process** has begun. He promises that **He will make us holy** in spirit, soul, and body as we trust in, believe in, abide in, and live His Word by the power of the Holy Spirit. As long as we are on the Earth, our spiritual transformations never cease.

**You are not who you were, and you are
not yet who you are going to be.**

People are comfortable being saved. Through the process of that, we become safe in being saved. **The purpose of your salvation is a complete transformation of your life—first in your spirit, then your soul, and then your body.** As you study and apply the Word and allow the Holy Spirit to flow through you, you progressively become who He intended you to be—to represent God on Earth in everything you do. The world needs to see God in you, through you—your words, deeds, and actions.

Every human being on Earth at this moment has an addiction. All of us are addicted to our thoughts. **Change will never enter your life until you change your thinking.** Only when we add action to our thoughts do we become productive. We create our lives (reality) by the action of our thoughts. Every action we take is birthed out of our thoughts, which create our desires. **Greater than our thoughts about our lives are God's thoughts about us.**

"O Lord, our God, no one can compare with You. Such wonderful

works and miracles are all found with You! And You think of us all the time with Your countless expressions of love—far exceeding our expectations!" (Psalm 40:5 TPT).

David is communing face-to-face with God in the Secret Place.

"In His shelter in the day of trouble, that's where you'll find me, for He hides me there in His holiness. He has smuggled me into His Secret Place, where I'm kept safe and secure—out of reach from all my enemies" (Psalm 27:5 TPT).

Translated from the original language, His Secret Place means His **secret Presence, the secret of His face.** When the Bible speaks of His Presence, it is powerfully undergirding and has the following impactful results on your life:

to fill up,

to pervade,

to permeate,

to overspread,

to be under the watchful eyes of,

and in the face of.

The idea is that His face is being turned toward someone in acceptance and favor-to be sufficient, sustained, and supportive. In His Secret Place, He sustains, supports, and energizes us. He reveals the depth of His thoughts toward us.

On His **couch**, in His Secret Place, He shares deep thoughts about **who we are, why we are, and what we are.** This is the process of transformation, rebuilding, and forming clay into a vessel of honor. It is **alignment** with His unchanging Spirit.

His thoughts about you are infinite possibilities filled with substance, energy, a higher level of living, and the ability to go **above and beyond.** His supreme purpose is to return us to the true essence and purpose of the life we were created for today. You are nothing less than a living, eternal, immortal thought of God. God thinks about you continuously, and His thoughts about you are always positive and good. **His greatest desire is for you to become His thoughts of you**.

> *"So will the words that come out of My mouth not come back empty-handed. They'll do the work I sent them to do, they'll complete the **assignment** I gave them"* (Isaiah 55:11 MSG).

In His Secret Place, God reveals Himself to us. As He speaks to and with us, His Spirit searches the depths and mysteries of Who He is, His plan, and His purpose.

God's thoughts of us reveal:

1. He has a **plan** for us.

2. His design for us is **wholeness**.

3. His plan **negates the harm** and evil Satan intends for us.

4. We are filled with **hope and a future when we accept these thoughts**.

Thoughts involve the process of designing a pattern or plan for an action, a device, or an invention. They involve imagination, a purpose that He has designed for you. They are like a wall protecting you, organizing your life. His thoughts are designed to **bring you wholeness and peace**. We become full, whole, and complete as we receive His thoughts in His Secret Place. The disciplines and disappointments of life are not without meaning and purpose. God uses everything that happens to us and within us to enrich our lives and cause His purposes to be fulfilled. When we live by His thoughts and abide by His plan and laws, our lives are filled with goodness, righteousness, power, and love.

Life in the Secret Place is an **educational process** where we learn about knowledge and understanding. They are twin anchors that help us journey through life.

Einstein said, "Any fool can know. The point is to understand."

Knowledge, coupled with understanding, is power. Power is only relevant if you use it wisely. **Knowledge brings information—understanding results in transformation**.

Our thoughts become God's thoughts and transform us into our true God-self. He then causes our plans to be established and to succeed. His thoughts become the seed of our lives. When we commit our ways and works to God, He takes responsibility for them, anchors them, and causes them to produce.

It is in His Secret Place that we enter into a covenant with Him.

"The secret [of the sweet, satisfying companionship] of the Lord have they who fear (revere and worship) Him, and He will show them His covenant and reveal to them its [deep, inner] meaning" (Psalm 25:14 AMPC).

We discover the deep inner meaning of knowing and living in covenant with Him. God commits to us the **Word of His covenant**. His Word energizes our thoughts with His life. When God speaks His Word and I receive and activate it by faith, it becomes a two-edged sword going to the depths of my being, exposing, sifting, analyzing, and judging the very thoughts and purposes of the heart.

"For we have the living Word of God, which is full of energy, and it pierces more sharply than a two-edged sword. It will even penetrate to the very core of our being where soul and spirit, bone and marrow meet! It interprets and reveals the true thoughts and secret motives of our hearts" (Hebrews 4:12 TPT).

Throughout the Bible, rest is a place of God's design. It is a

spiritual principle to always be in a responding mode to God's initiative.

His design is not a delightful take-it-or-leave-it option but rather a mandate for acquisition.

His design fulfills our highest identity and development. **Rest** means to be at **His place**, in **His time**, **doing** what He has planned for us, confident in His strength and resources. This process occurs in His Secret Place, where we find rest. We think His thoughts, discover His strategy, submit to His timing, and appropriate His resources through our encounter with Him.

He invites us to join Him in the Secret Place on His couch to be recreated in His image. Man's **highest potential** and most fulfilling function are realized as he abides in the Secret Place of the Most High God. Man is dependent on God for His continued existence. Life in the Secret Place is life in the **Fourth Dimension**. There is a transformation of spirit, soul, body. Man realizes his **ultimate being** as he sits in God's Presence and is transformed into the image and likeness for which God created him.

"It is through Him that we live and function and have our identity; just as your own poets have said, 'Our lineage comes from Him'" (Acts 17:28 TPT).

"What I'm getting at, friends, is that you should simply keep on doing what you've done from the beginning. When I was living among you, you lived in responsive obedience. Now that I'm separated from you, keep it up. Better yet, redouble your efforts. Be energetic in your life of salvation, reverent and sensitive before God. That energy is God's energy, an energy deep within you, God Himself willing and working at what will give Him the most pleasure" (Philippians 2:12-13 MSG).

He created us for Himself. We function best when fully alive in Him—totally surrendered to His will and ways. Man, as he came from the hands of His Creator, was whole, complete, possessed integrity and innocence—literally, he was holy. **Man is God's highest creation**—an **image-bearer** of God. Even though man fell into sin, he still bears God's image, which is being restored in Jesus' atoning work on the Cross.

"God knew what He was doing from the very beginning. He decided from the outset to shape the lives of those who love Him along the same lines as the life of His Son. The Son stands first in the line of humanity He restored. We see the original and intended shape of our lives there in Him" (Romans 8:29 MSG).

You and I are to enter His Secret Place, sit in His Presence (glory), and reflect like a mirror Who He is in and through us to the world around us.

A great law of life says that we become like who and what we live with.

In His Secret Place, His image and likeness are restored to us. The more we become like Him, the more we rule in life with His Presence in us. God has never given up on the quest to have sons and daughters on Earth who act, think, and behave like Him.

"The entire Universe is standing on tiptoe, yearning to see the unveiling of God's glorious sons and daughters!" (Romans 8:19 TPT).

Man can only know His greatness in relationship to God. When He reveals Himself, He reveals us at the same time. Made in His image and His likeness, man was **able not to sin.** As he was created, he was not yet a finished product. He still needed the daily visits in the Garden to grow in the knowledge and wisdom of His Creator.

Adam and Eve disobeyed God's command because of the sin of unbelief. The image of God in man was perverted, corrupted, and deformed and needed to be restored and renewed. The **renewal of His image** means we are to live in **responsive obedience** to His Word and His Spirit. We think God's thoughts after Him and use our volitional powers to will what He wants to accomplish in and through us. God's answer to the question: *What is man?* is summed up in these words:

Man is a living, breathing human being recreated in My likeness, a product of My divine power.

The significance of this powerful Truth is that God remakes us and restores His image in us, and we ultimately become our true God-selves. The result of accepting that powerful Truth should define our human life and deliver us from every satanic attack, character assassination, unworthy thought, and every ungodly act.

According to Psalm 8:5, God remembers us, attends to us, and endlessly observes us. **As long as you have breath and consciousness, He will make every effort to recreate you in the image of His Son.**

All of this is necessary because sin has fractured, injured, scarred, and marred His image in us. However, God is never caught off guard by the enemy's attack. From the beginning, God issued a **divine decree**: *Before you entered your mother's womb, He had perfected a specific plan for your life (Psalm 139).*

Only by regularly sitting in council with God in His Secret Place will you be equipped to live your God-life—**The Fourth Dimension.**

"Lay aside your old Adam-self with its masquerade and disguise. For you have acquired new creation life which is continually being renewed into the likeness of the One Who

created you; giving you the full revelation of God" (Colossians 3:9-10 TPT).

God's desire for mankind is a full and complete restoration of the entire being— spirit, soul, body. **Holiness** is His plan for us—to be **whole, complete, lacking nothing.**

"The Lord will perfect that which concerns me..." (Psalm 138:8 AMPC).

The word **perfect** means to **complete, finish,** and **perform.** God will perfect and complete His purpose in us as we continually abide with Him in His Secret Place.

Again, we are speaking of **whole life transformation**—spirit, soul, body. His intent for each of us is not a visitation to the Secret Place but a habitation—**there I become the real me.**

Jesus came to give us a Kingdom and teach us its operation. He gave us His Church as the agency of that Kingdom. His purpose was the education of our spirits, our humanity—to become citizens of His Kingdom. Our goal is to live out the laws of His Kingdom through the operation of His Church. Unfortunately, man's will to build the church has overshadowed the building of the Kingdom. We must never forget that Jesus came to give us a Kingdom. He said, *"I will build My Church."* In that sense, we should focus on preaching the Gospel of the Kingdom as He builds His Church.

Keys to Activate Your Kingdom Destiny

Chapter 4

 There, I am blessed with inner gladness based on a spiritual reality.

 In the Secret Place, I determine who God created me to be.

 In the Secret Place, God gives me His counsel.

 The Secret Place is a picture of me sitting on God's couch, hearing His covenant.

 In the Secret Place, I not only learn who He is, but I also learn who I am.

 In the Secret Place, I learn God's thoughts of me.

 There, He aligns me with who I am, why I am, and what I am.

 In the Secret Place, I receive knowledge that results in transformation.

 In the Secret Place, I experience the renewal of His image and His likeness in me.

The Kingdom: **Greater than the Church**

ALL over the Federal buildings and monuments in Washington, quotes from the Bible are etched in stone. Obviously, our founding fathers wanted everyone to know that from our beginnings, we were a country influenced by the Judeo-Christian teachings of God's Word. The two listed below are found on the walls of our Federal buildings.

> "*Wisdom is the principal thing; therefore, get wisdom and with all thy getting, get understanding*" (Proverbs 4:7).

> "*What doth the Lord require of thee, but to do justly, and to love mercy, and to walk humbly with thy God*" (Micah 6:8).

Government and the media are, for the most part, liberal and intolerant of the Christian faith. Many of the edicts coming from Washington are not only anti-God, they appear demonic at their source. Our moral climate is rotten to the core. The LGBTQ influence on our federal government has reached a new low with the emphasis on homosexual marriage and transgenderism. Both of these are an affront to the Biblical teachings and are fed by an anti-Christ spirit. Because America is the land of the free, people have the right to choose their lifestyle. However, the government should stay out of those personal choices.

America is the greatest, wealthiest nation in the world. Our currency reads: **In God we Trust**. We have more churches per capita than any other country. America has more Bibles, Christian literature, and Christian schools than any other nation. Yet, America has incessantly turned away from God, His Kingdom rule, and His Holy Spirit. The church seems impotent to "flesh out" His life in ours and impart His vision, character, and values. When a church is not manifesting the Kingdom of God (its laws and wisdom), it loses its power to influence transformation in people's lives. It is more man-centered than Kingdom-centered.

Freedom and prosperity have inherent dangers. While teaching God's Word produces both, we must be careful of the comfort and pleasure of the **good life**. With them comes the temptation to trust our blessings rather than the Blesser. God warned Israel against forgetting the Lord as their source of salvation and freedom. Nine times in Deuteronomy, He tells them not to forget what He has done for them and reminds them 15 times of how He delivered them from slavery and bondage.

> *"Tell those rich in this world's wealth to quit being so full of themselves and so obsessed with money, which is here today and gone tomorrow. Tell them to go after God, Who piles on all the riches we could ever manage — to do good, to be rich in helping others, to be extravagantly generous. If they do that, they'll build a treasury that will last, gaining life that is truly life"* (1 Timothy 6:17-19 MSG).

In His message to the Laodicean church *(Revelation 3:14-18)*, the

Lord warns against the deadening and lukewarm effects of trusting in material wealth rather than pursuing a vital faith relationship with Jesus Christ. (This occurs when we are more church-minded than Kingdom-minded.) The church had lost its ability to impact its world because it had become preoccupied with material comforts, pleasure, and prosperity. They left Christ standing outside—closing the door to His Presence. (Perhaps this is why Jesus says, *"Behold I stand at the door and knock"* in Revelation 3:20.)

Laodicea was a wealthy, commercial, financial banking center. It had a medical center known for its ointment for treating ears and a powder to make a salve for the eyes. It was famous for providing black wool and mass-producing garments. Laodicea means **people ruling**. They were so rich and independent that after an earthquake, they refused help from Rome to rebuild.

Many rebuilt structures included the inscription—**"Out of our own resources."** They did have one inadequacy—their lack of a water supply. They ran an aqueduct coming from a spring four miles to the south. Thus, their water was lukewarm.

Jesus condemns **four** things in this church that caused them to lose their Kingdom-mindedness. These things can be easily said about many churches in our day.

1. **Indifferent**: Lukewarm, neither hot nor cold. A lukewarm person lacks enthusiasm and is half-hearted, without true conviction and commitment, lacking the Holy Spirit's passion, fire, and zeal.

2. **Prideful**: They said we are rich and need nothing.

3. **Self-deceived**: They did not know their real condition.

4. **Spiritual poverty**: Wretched, miserable, poor, blind and naked.

This church was hardened against God's Truth and lacked spiritual insight and discernment. They were void of a Biblical perspective or vision, and the eyes of their hearts were not enlightened. They had not clothed themselves with the garments of His Word, His Spirit, His power.

Though they had an ointment for their physical eyes, they were spiritually blind to God and His ways. Periodically, some movements arise in the church that make things more palatable for the culture because it is something new and less intrusive. They are not so much in your face, and the message is somewhat watered down. Those movements flourish only for a season since they lack the in-depth teaching of His Kingdom. In the softening of the message, they take away the power of it. Jesus Himself called many of the religious leaders of His day, specifically the Pharisees and Sadducees, hypocrites and vipers because they failed to emphasize the true Gospel. Paul speaks of people with itching ears *(2 Timothy 4:3-4 MSG)*. A failure to emphasize the power of the Gospel of Jesus Christ, the Truth as it is in Jesus, results in few signs, wonders, and miracles. **A diluted Gospel produces polluted results**.

But in His love, His counsel, He offers a remedy. He counsels them and offers **true** riches—refined gold, white raiment, eye salve. Put on My Word, the Fruit of My Spirit, the Garment of Righteousness, and Joy in the Holy Spirit.

"...So be enthusiastic and in earnest and burning with zeal and repent..." (Revelation 3:19 AMPC).

To the church at Ephesus, these compelling words were written:

*"But I have this [one charge to make] against you: that **you have left (abandoned) the love that you had at first** [you have deserted Me, your first love]" (Revelation 2:4 AMPC).*

It can indeed be said of America and its many churches that we have left the love we once had for God and His Kingdom upon which our nation was founded. That abandoned love created the seeds of discord, racism, intolerance, strife, and conflict. Love always is a uniting force, especially His love.

Love is said to be the most powerful force in the world.

It is never about how much love you have in your life— it's about how much life you have in your love.

You can live without loving, but you cannot love without living. Pray that you become the reason someone experiences love, God's love.

He first loved us (1 John 4:19).

"For God so loved us He gave His only begotten Son" (John 3:16).

Love is the ultimate law of the Universe, the law of God's very being. Accepting the Christian Law of Love is the realization that we must live in harmony with the Being of God, and His Being is love. Every human being is created for no other reason than His love. His love says we are redeemable, made for sonship, fellowship, and communion with Him. It is from Him that we receive the meaning of love.

Love is, first of all, a relationship. It is the result of a dynamic and growing relationship with Jesus Christ.

We are created **by** love, **for** love, **in** love, **to** love.

As believers, we live to love others with God's love. The primary motivation of the Christian life is love. *"Love never fails" (1 Corinthians 13:8).*

However, Jesus commended the Church at Ephesus for their many virtues. This was a large and very prosperous city of between

250,000 and 500,000 people. The Temple of Diana was located there and was one of the seven wonders of the ancient world. It was more than two football fields in length. Immorality, religious prostitution, and demonic rituals flourished there. The Apostle Paul founded the church there and spent three years ministering in the surrounding area. Priscilla, Aquila, and Apollos brought the Gospel to the city prior to Paul's arrival. Timothy served as pastor, and John was an elder there.

No church in history had as rich a heritage as this large, busy, prominent church. Yet they had a glaring weakness despite their witness. They had left their first love. Jesus had their heads and their hands but not their hearts. They consciously left, abandoning their passionate love for Jesus. The danger of a love grown cold includes indifference, apathy, lack of interest, and lack of concern. It is more concern for the work of God than for the God of the work. Many are more willing to **build a Temple** for God than to **be a Temple of God**.

The Christian life is either a passionate love affair with Jesus or nothing. **First Love is fervent, emotional, fresh, alive, and vibrant**. It moves the heart. **First Love is extravagant**—you can't get enough of Him—His Word—His Spirit—His Presence. You can't do enough for Him, His Kingdom. Serving Him is a joy. Witnessing for Him is continuous.

> *"Remember then from what heights you have fallen. Repent and do the works you did previously [when first you knew the Lord]..." (Revelation 2:5 AMPC).*

Love, spirit-life, and spiritual power are always missing when the church abandons the message of the Kingdom. It becomes evident in the letters to the seven churches of Asia that they have abandoned the messages of His Kingdom. It seems as though **the churches had become institutions rather than living organisms**.

What the world needs more than ever is a **church** with a **Kingdom perspective**. His Kingdom is manifested through us as we develop our prayer life. It was Jesus Himself Who taught us to pray like this: *Your Kingdom come. Seek first His Kingdom and His righteousness.*

In Revelation 2, He said the church is to be a

praying church

giving church

serving church

witnessing church

Prayer is man's highest **privilege** and greatest **duty**. It is in prayer that we experience **His Presence**. Prayer is the only way we access God's heart for His Kingdom work on Earth, accomplished through His Church.

God shapes the world by prayer. **Prayer is a disinfectant and a preventative**. It purifies the air and destroys the contagion of evil. The degree of God's Presence on Earth corresponds to the degree of our prayers. Prayer puts God in full force in the world, the church, and our lives.

"Since before time began no one has ever imagined, no ear heard, no eye seen, a God like You Who works for those who wait for Him" (Isaiah 64:4 MSG).

God has obligated Himself to answer prayer. Our prayers put God to work in our human affairs. Prayer produces action in the divine, the angelic, and the human realm.

- God is moved to action according to His will.

- Angels are assigned on errands of mercy and as messengers of hope.

- Humans respond with spiritual acts of supernatural power.

Prayer is an appeal to God, communication with God, and intimate communion with Him. Prayer is an activity whereby we seek His face while opening our hearts and will to His promised guidance and help. **Prayer is an exercise in which we aim to avail ourselves of those spiritual resources God has mandated to all who seek His will.** It is asking God to fulfill His needs and will through us. There is no prayer without total surrender to His will and ways. Prayer makes us available to carry out and accomplish His plans and purposes for His Kingdom on Earth to the fullest.

"For you have need of steadfast patience and endurance, so that you may perform and fully accomplish the will of God, and thus receive and carry away [and enjoy to the full] what is promised" (Hebrews 10:36 AMPC).

Simply put—prayer works.

The question is—How do we pray?

The disciples watched Jesus go away alone and pray often. Finally, they requested of Him—*"Lord, teach us to pray" (Luke 11:1 NIV).*

"And He said to them, When you pray, say: 'Our Father Who is in Heaven, hallowed be Your Name, Your Kingdom come. Your will be done [held holy and revered] on Earth as it is in Heaven'" (Luke 11:2 AMPC).

With Jesus, His Father was always *first*. His first recorded words are found in Luke 2:49. Jesus remained in Jerusalem after the Feast of Passover, but His parents were unaware of this.

They searched for Him for three days and found Him in the court of the Temple, sitting among the teachers. They chastised Him for not telling them.

> *"And He said to them, 'How is it that you had to look for Me? Did you not see and know that it is necessary [as a duty] for Me to be in My Father's house and [occupied] about My Father's business?'" (Luke 2:49 AMPC).*

And in His last utterance before His death on the Cross, He addresses His Father—*"Father, into Your hands I commit My spirit!" (Luke 23:46 AMPC).*

In this prayer, Jesus' initial focus is upward, with its first three requests concerning the Father's glory and the last three with man.

God first, then man. His glory before our needs. Notice that we are to pray to God, our Father—not to Jesus or the Holy Spirit, but to God.

The word **father** comes from a root meaning
nourisher, protector, upholder—one who imparts life,
brings it into being, and passes on the potential for likeness.

Knowing God as our Father is a sign of our spiritual health and of the authenticity of our faith and is one of the most healing doctrines in all of Scripture.

Maybe you grew up without a father, or he passed away at an early age, or your relationship with him was negative. Yet you desire a father's touch, affirmation, and acceptance. You can find wholeness and healing as God, our Father, loves, accepts, and affirms us. Wounded by a sense of sin, the conscience finds healing in His loving arms.

Desire is **fulfilled.**
Distrust finds **confidence.**
Depression finds **joy.**
Ignorance is **enlightened.**

Poverty finds **provision.**
Weakness finds **strength.**
Darkness is changed to **light.**
Fear is **vanished.**
Hope is **restored.**

Prayer is to a Father with a Father's heart, a Father's love, a Father's strength. God is this kind of Father. In prayer, you bond with the God of the Universe, your Father. As a Father, He freely gives us all things. His gifts are manifold, and they equip our lives for Kingdom service.

"Every good gift and every perfect (free, large, full) gift is from above; it comes down from the Father of all [that gives] light" (James 1:17 AMPC).

One of the ways God manifests Himself in His Kingdom on Earth is through His laws and by empowering His children with special endowments called gifts. As we operate according to His Kingdom laws and manifest His gifts in our daily living, the Kingdom is advanced on Earth. God is forever the great giver. Everything He created gives.

The sun gives.
The moon gives.
The stars give.
The rain gives.
The ground gives.
Trees give.
Plants give.
Animals give.

You and I are the physical and spiritual extension of the life and ministry of Jesus on the Earth by the power of His Holy Spirit and His gifts. By the power of the Holy Spirit, He gifts and graces us with many spiritual gifts so His wisdom, knowledge, miracles, power, love, salvation, healing, and deliverance would be manifested throughout the Earth. As believers, we no longer live for ourselves but for Him Who died and rose again on our behalf.

"And He died for all, so that all those who live might live no longer to and for themselves, but to and for Him Who died and was raised again for their sake" (2 Corinthians 5:15 AMPC).

God has given every believer at least one gift. A spiritual gift is a God-given ability for service in His Kingdom on Earth. Your gift is revealed and confirmed as you grow in Christ and serve Him through His Kingdom plan and purpose. Your gift must be exercised and developed. God Himself determines which gift(s) you are given for service to His Kingdom. Any spiritual gift not taken "through the Cross" can never reach its full potential.

"A man's gift makes room for him and brings him before great men" (Proverbs 18:16 AMPC).

**You are not to make room for your gift—
your gift will make room for you.**

The exercise of your spiritual giftedness must flow out of your Godliness. God never calls us primarily to a task—He calls us unto Himself. Before I can do something for God, I must become someone in relationship with God. Our **work** for Him will never exceed our **walk** with Him. We become aware of our true God-self from our walk with Him. You will never be great for Christ until you are great with Christ.

**You become invincible in your Kingdom service
when you discover your identity and experience
your uniqueness (which you are gifted for).**

Everything you need to become significantly successful—virtues, qualities, strengths—is already within you, waiting to be released. Powers, potentialities, and possibilities are latent within us, but they are undeveloped and imprisoned by our fears, doubts, and lack of pursuit. Surrender to your God-given talents and gifts and take them through His Cross; you will discover His provision and power there. No spiritual gift can ever be perfected in our fleshly beings. **Each gift must be utilized according to the proportion of our faith.**

"Having gifts (faculties, talents, qualities) that differ according to the grace given us, let us use them: [He whose gift is] prophecy, [let him prophesy] according to the proportion of his faith" (Romans 12:6 AMPC).

Every morning, you should remind yourself that God has equipped you today with His power to go out and **make a life** (rather than make a living) with the gift(s) He has deposited within you. **We should not neglect the gift in us but stir it up (rekindle the embers, fan the flame, and keep it burning hot).** Give Him your gift(s), and watch Him use you in ways you never dreamed could happen. One of the greatest hindrances to the manifestation of the Kingdom on Earth is the failure of believers to exercise their gift(s). Through those Kingdom gifts, we come to know our true God-self and operate in the power and Presence of the Holy Spirit's anointing. **Our gifts are loaned** to us while on Earth to **build His Kingdom** as they enrich and fulfill our lives.

Perhaps it may come as a surprise that nowhere in the New Testament are we, as believers, ministers commanded to **build the church.** In fact, there is a "Gospel of the Kingdom" (Matthew 4:23, Matthew 9:35, Matthew 24:14, Mark 1:14), but there is no "gospel of the church." Jesus only used the word **church** twice, but He referred to the **Kingdom** more than a hundred times in the Gospels, emphasizing the **Kingdom is greater than the Church.**

Just as surprising is Jesus' own statement,

"I will build My Church" (Matthew 16:18).

In *Acts 2:47*, Luke says,

"And the Lord added to their number daily those who were being saved" (NIV).

Paul further emphasizes this principle in *1 Corinthians 3:6*—

"I have planted, Apollos watered; but God gave the increase" (KJV).

While thousands of books, podcasts, seminars, and church growth specialists proclaim how man can build the church, God's Word declares that only Jesus can accomplish the task. In the New Testament, there are many great Kingdom growth principles. Our assignment as believers is to **preach the Gospel of the Kingdom**, and Jesus will build His Church. Man can indeed build **a** church, and many have done so. Our focus on **church growth** could be part of the reason why the church has lost its appeal to many unchurched people who refer to it as boring, irrelevant, religious, and judgmental. No such statements could ever truthfully be said about the Kingdom!

Man often rules and reigns in the church. Whether in a local entity or a denominational setting, men often allow their egos, flesh, and carnal spirits to influence their decisions. In His Kingdom, the Holy Spirit is the **Chief Executive Officer** and the **Chief Operating Officer**. As CEO, He decides what is to be done. As COO, He carries out the mission in partnership with believers. God created each of us to function in a conscious, intimate relationship of interactive responsibility with Him and equipped us for one uniting purpose— to build His Kingdom on Earth.

The church often separates and divides us along denominational, theological, and racial differences. Through a process of renewal,

God generously loves us and patiently leads us from our carnal, fleshly perspective into our true Kingdom identity—sons and daughters of the one true God. Every living thing is created to live within its natural habitat. What it is dictates its world. Move it out of its unique environment, and it struggles or dies.

Fish are made to live in water, some in fresh water and some in salt water. Animals are made to live on land. If you place fish on land, they die. If you place animals underwater, they die. Likewise, when believers live as merely soul-body entities instead of **spirit-beings**, we live outside our natural habitat. Our created design is to live as spiritual beings in His **spiritual Kingdom**.

The Kingdom is greater than the church—always. We must become more Kingdom-minded and less church-focused to reach God's desired harvest.

The amazing genius Albert Einstein said, "Any fool can know. The point is to understand." To understand is to perceive. **Perception becomes reality**. When you understand something, you no longer fear it.

Love requires acceptance, affirmation, and understanding.
Oneness demands understanding.
Intimacy breeds understanding.
All humanity desires to understand and to be understood.

The Law of Understanding helps us to decipher the difference between the Kingdom and the church. Lack of understanding is the world's greatest cause of conflict. Understanding produces trust. No wonder the wise man Solomon said, *"In all of your getting, get understanding."* The Hebrew word means to **build**. To build or construct something, one must be able to plan and grasp the processes necessary for success. Understanding is born in the heart—the emotional seat of man.

"Trust in the LORD with all your heart, and lean not on your own understanding" (Proverbs 3:5 NKJV).

Understanding has a source—God. Understanding has a residence—the heart. Understanding is expressed through an attitude. Nothing is more critical and lacking in the Christian life than **spiritual understanding.** Only when we understand how His Kingdom operates do we understand the meaning and purpose of human existence.

Paul prayed for the church (and us) at Ephesus to have spiritual understanding: *"The eyes of your understanding being enlightened..." (Ephesians 1:18 NKJV).*

"Life was in Him, life that made sense of human existence" (John 1:4 Literal Translation).

Each of us has a "kingdom." It's a **realm** uniquely our own, where our choices determine our destiny. We must understand that each of us is created to "have dominion." It is how God formed us—to rule, reign, and be like Him—image and likeness.

**We are never-ceasing, spiritual beings
with a unique eternal calling to participate with God
in ruling His Kingdom on Earth.**

God has placed a piece of Himself within each of us (*Genesis 2:7*), and only when we willingly invite Him to rule in us and through us with His mighty Kingdom laws is it possible for us to be fulfilled. Anyone without God's Presence always has a sense of incompleteness, a knowing that something is missing. At some point, everyone desires God, whether or not they acknowledge it. **He wants us to understand our creation covenant.** We are assigned collectively with differing gifts, talents, and abilities to rule with Him over all living things on Earth. That is our responsibility, our job description.

As we submit to Him, our understanding of His Kingdom grows within us, and our rule and dominion increase in life. *"In all your getting, get understanding."* Then, you will be **equipped** to **build** your life by exercising His Kingdom's laws.

The Kingdom laws determine the functionality of the Kingdom. And with that functionality, the Kingdom becomes activated as we use our gifts to serve Him and His Kingdom.

Imagine what our world would look like if we activated our Kingdom gifts to serve Him.

No one is ever qualified to lead who doesn't understand how to serve. Greatness, significance, position, power, influence—these and many other words define a successful life. Millions worldwide seek to get ahead, get to the top, and make a better life. We often speak of such people as "go-getters," "achievers," "rising stars," "movers and shakers," "driven," "ambitious," "leaders," etc. That is how the world defines "who" we must be to succeed.

He who will get ahead, rise to the top, lead, flourish, and gain influence is he who is willing to serve others. His disciples had no will of their own, no business of their own, and were living solely for their master, Jesus Christ, dependent upon and obedient to Him. It describes a servant who willingly commits to serve a master he loves and respects. The bondservant's every thought, breath, and effort was subject to the will of his master.

The foundation for knowing the abiding joy of the Lord is to recognize and submit to Jesus as your **Owner and Master**. He alone has the right to command how and where you should live, how you should spend your time and money, and even what thoughts you should dwell on. After all, we are serving Him in His Kingdom—not just serving the church.

At some point, we all die. The big question is, **"Will you live before you die?"** Within each of us, there is the power to live our lives daily, which we all do. However, there is also your **unlived life**—subconscious, unconscious—that contains hopes, dreams, aspirations, and desires that you have never fully expressed in your living. **Day by day, you should be concerned with your lived life and your unlived one.** Perhaps Paul gave us the proper sentence to address this: *"This one thing I do."* You must decide what it is in your unlived life that is absolutely necessary for you to live. **Only as Christ lives in me and through me will I experience what it is to really live me.**

Only God can reveal to you who you truly are. We must first believe that God is Who He says He is before we can accept who He says we are. If you ever come to know your true God-self, you will never settle for being someone else. When you fall, you get up, ask God for forgiveness, and move on in your **God-assigned purpose.** You intensely **pursue** His **Presence** so you may experience His power. This is one of the most misunderstood relationships in His Kingdom. We don't like the concept of being a servant. It goes against our independence. In our culture, freedom is the right to do as one pleases.

The message of the Kingdom is all about servanthood and the freedom granted to us by a relationship with Jesus Christ. Often, the church can be a very limiting culture while the Kingdom is unlimited. In the Bible, freedom is the privilege to do the will of the Father—I exchange my life for the life of Jesus Christ through me. In that exchange, He promises **pardon, power,** and **partnership.**

Pardon means forgiveness from past sins, freedom from the law of sin and death, and a passionate **desire** never to sin again.

"For you have died, and your [new, real] life is hidden with Christ in God" (Colossians 3:3 AMPC).

Power comes to us as we **yield** our will to His will—become His Kingdom servants. Our **will** becomes dominated by the **mind of Christ**. We no longer live out of our resources; Christ lives through us, and His power sustains us.

Partnership brings **oneness** with Him in life and death.

"...For His sake I have lost everything and consider it all to be mere rubbish, in order that I may win (gain) Christ... [For my determined purpose is] that I may know Him and that I may in that same way come to know the power outflowing from His resurrection, and that I may so share His sufferings as to be continually transformed to His death, that if possible I may attain to the resurrection out from among the dead" (Philippians 3:8, 10-11 AMPC).

God's **highest purpose** for our lives—**our spiritual destiny activated**—is most fully realized when we begin to live our true Kingdom God-designed life.

We are encouraged to *"Let this same attitude and purpose and [humble] mind be in you which was in Christ Jesus..."* (Philippians 2:5 AMPC).

The Kingdom is always about the education of our spirits. Often, the church focuses on the education of our minds. A mind is a terrible thing to waste. God gives us a brain, and then we create our minds. "Thoughts" are simply the activity of the mind. The arena of the uncrucified thought-life is the battleground of the enemy's attack on our lives.

"For as he thinks in his heart, so is he" (Proverbs 23:7 AMPC).

The greatest position of a believer in God's Kingdom is to become more like Jesus. His mind must be disciplined to know Christ and live to serve Him only. It is the place where thoughts are birthed, and the will is engaged. **Mind is the realm of perception, understanding, feeling, desire, and will.**

He must be *"renewed in the spirit of his mind"* (Ephesians 4:23).

A **transformed mind** equips us to *"refute arguments, theories, reasonings and every proud and lofty thing that sets itself up against the [true] knowledge of God; and we lead every thought and purpose away captive into the obedience of Christ..."* (2 Corinthians 10:5 AMPC).

We are to **destroy fortresses, overthrow strongholds**. A **stronghold** is a demonically-induced pattern of thinking-any type of thinking that exalts itself above God's Truth, giving the enemy a place of influence in our thought life. A negative mindset will cause you to become a **SPOW—Spiritual Prisoner of War**.

You will never experience a transformed mind until you experience a transformed spirit. Jesus came into our world to educate us about His Kingdom's glory, power, authority, and anointing. The more we know and understand His Kingdom, the greater our effectiveness in the church.

"For You did form my inward parts; You did knit me together in my mother's womb" (Psalm 139:13).

Inward parts refer to the **secret chambers of our inner being**. God has your true spiritual DNA inside your spirit—who you are in His Kingdom. As you live, a demand will be made on those things hidden for the advancement of His Kingdom.

Noah is a perfect example of this spiritual fact. When he was 500 years old, God instructed him to build an ark. No one had ever built an ark. No drawings, skills, or tools were available for such an enormous task. But before Noah was conceived in his mother's womb, God knew that the world would demand an ark one day. God would need Noah to complete that task. Until the demand came, Noah had no idea what he was capable of. The Ark has to be one of the Biblical wonders of the world because of its construction, functionality, and durability. This is the God we serve! What is hidden inside *your* spiritual wallet? This was true of Noah and many of the main characters in God's Word. God constantly surprises us with who He created us to be.

Life's greatest joy is the discovery and experience of our **God-assigned identity**, which helps us focus on our purpose. Every entertained thought, every experienced emotion, and every behavior are statements about who I am and who I am becoming. **My spiritual destiny is activated as I understand my highest purpose is to know the Lord God personally and intimately and to serve and obey Him with all my heart.** He deserves to be served with all the energy and passion I am capable of.

Nothing ignites your passion like serving Him with your gift. On a continuing basis, we must stir up and fan into a flame the gift He has placed within us. I am most productive when I bring my **highest self**—spirit, soul, body—to any activity. You and I are to offer our lives to God as fuel for the flame which energizes His Kingdom on Earth. We then serve Him through the passion of our hearts. Our gift must be used to serve Him to reach our highest level of spiritual productivity. We should not be shy, passive, or fearful in our service to Him.

"For God did not give us a spirit of timidity or cowardice or fear, but [He has given us a spirit] of power and of love and of

sound judgment and personal discipline [abilities that result in a calm, well-balanced mind and self-control]" (2 Timothy 1:7 AMP).

Paul was in his late sixties, but his body bore the marks of much suffering. He was in a cold, damp dungeon in Rome about A.D. 67, awaiting execution at the hands of Nero. He could have been discouraged.

He grieved that the day would come when professing Christians would not endure sound doctrine but would pile up teachers to tickle their ears, turning from the truth to myths. But Paul was stirred with passion as he encouraged the shy, timid Timothy to stir up and fan into a flame his spiritual gift.

God will give you a fullness of His power and His love, and He will give you a disciplined mind. Your gift exercised will cause you to triumph. We add value to our Kingdom life by focusing on using our gifts and exercising them passionately. God is an investor. He is always concerned that what He invests in will result in an excellent return—a **KROI—Kingdom Return on Investment**.

His **investment principle** is found in this passage:

"...For everyone to whom much is given, of him shall much be required..." (Luke 12:48 AMPC).

Our assignment is to take what He has invested in us and invest in others. One day, He will hold each of us accountable.

"Sooner or later we'll all have to face God, regardless of our conditions. We will appear before Christ and take what's coming to us as a result of our actions, either good or bad" (2 Corinthians 5:10 MSG).

Spiritual investments are His highest, most valuable investments in us. Gifts, talents, abilities, resources, money, and opportunities are entrusted to us by God, and He expects us to manage them well as His stewards. When we are faithful in our stewardship and service to Him and His Kingdom, He rewards us according to our works for Him—works He designed for us and designed us for.

"For we are God's [own] handiwork (His workmanship), recreated in Christ Jesus, [born anew] that we may do those good works which God predestined (planned beforehand) for us [taking paths which He prepared ahead of time], that we should walk in them [living the good life which He prearranged and made ready for us to live]" (Ephesians 2:10 AMPC).

Some will have their works burned up, destroyed—

"But if any person's work is burned up [under the test], he will suffer the loss [of it all, losing his reward], though he himself will be saved, but only as [one who has passed] through fire" (1 Corinthians 3:15 AMPC).

Perhaps this is why there are tears in Heaven. At times on Earth, we lived half-heartedly, complaining, just going through the motions, failing to witness to others, and not fully supporting His Kingdoms with tithes—we have tears for lives lived for ourselves rather than for His Kingdom.

Thank God He will take care of our tears:

"...and God will wipe away every tear from their eyes" (Revelation 7:17 AMPC).

God is both our reward and our Rewarder. He will **reward** His faithful ones. You don't have to **enter His Presence** empty-handed.

He wants us to receive our just rewards. He will reveal His plans to us, and He is willing to *"make all grace (every favor and earthly blessing) come to you in abundance, so that you may always and under all circumstances and whatever the need be self-sufficient [possessing enough to require no aid or support and furnished in abundance for every good work and charitable donation]" (2 Corinthians 9:8 AMPC).*

What is my **Kingdom purpose** in life?

How do I achieve and live my **highest life**?

Our life is an investment by God from which we are to create our God-life. On the one hand, life is a struggle—the survival of the fittest.

The Bible uses two different words for "life." One is the life of **circumstance** or environment—transient and changing, the present state of existence. The other is a life that has a sense of **eternity** in it, a God-kind of life. God did not design life to **break** you; He designed it to **make** you.

There is a difference between **existence and life.** A stone exists and lasts, but it does not live. Real life is life crowned with glory and honor. It is an approved life, a rewarded life. God wants to reward us here with long life, health, joyfulness, peace, and an eternity with crowns of rejoicing and glory. The rewarded life is the **Fourth Dimension** life. It is a God-honoring life of righteousness, peace, and joy in the Holy Spirit. It is Kingdom life here and in eternity. It is promised to us by God.

"For you have need of steadfast patience and endurance, so that you may perform and fully accomplish the will of God, and thus receive and carry away [and enjoy to the full] what is promised" (Hebrews 10:36 AMPC).

As believers, we must take the long view of life—I call it the **Eternity Perspective.** Paul only lived his life in the present and with an eye towards the future—never the past. So should we. His life was filled with hope and much joy because of that attitude.

Hope is confident expectation of good. Joy is an attitude of cheerfulness and gladness and is a gift from God. Hope lifts us, and joy strengthens us. He organizes our lives so that we meet people who need God daily. Serve the King, care about others, and **share** the Good News as you journey through this earthly life.

At some point in the church, we stopped calling Christians disciples and started calling them believers.

A disciple serves and imitates Jesus. He loses his life in order to find it. He immerses himself in the language and culture of Christ until His Word **reshapes** him, **redefines** him, and **transforms** him from the inside to the outside—how he thinks, sees, dreams, and lives.

A believer holds certain beliefs, but how deeply they penetrate his life depends on his moods, circumstances, and challenges. You can't be a disciple without being a believer. You can be a casual follower of Jesus and not a disciple. We don't always live our beliefs.

The Kingdom is full of disciples, but our churches are filled with believers.

Believers desire information about God, His Kingdom, His acts, and His ability to meet their felt needs. They seek God's hand. Often, people lift their hands with palms extended up to receive from God rather than lifting them in total surrender in obedience to His will. It's the difference between "Bless me, oh Lord," and "I bless Your Name."

Disciples desire transformation. They seek God's face. Rather than asking God for what they need, they ask what **He needs** from them. **Living in the Fourth Dimension,** we die out to ourselves to come alive to Him—His plans, His purposes, His destiny for us. We live the Kingdom life.

God's glory transforms us as we continue to fill our lives with His Word. We become brighter and more influential as God perfects us in His likeness. The splendor of His glory increases within us from the inside to the outside. Transformation occurs only when we study His Word, not to meet some need in our lives, but to see His face. Man is interested in imparting information, not the intimacy of communication with the Word made flesh. We often want insight and information on how to process a problem, deal with a difficulty, and confront a circumstance.

We forget He said, *"Seek first My Kingdom and My righteousness and all these other things will be given to you" (Matthew 6:33).* All your human needs and concerns will be taken care of.

We must value **life transformation** more than just information. God's ultimate goal for **revealing His glory** is that **we are conformed to the image of His Son.** It is while **beholding Him in His Word** that His Word transforms us. God is His Word, and His Word contains His Presence.

Psychologists have discovered a trend in human relationships called integration. It is a marked tendency for mutual assimilation between persons who love each other (such as a husband and wife), are constantly in each other's presence, and are under each other's influence. They start to look alike, act alike, and complete each other's sentences. If you spend quality time in the presence of someone over a lengthy period of time, you will have a measure of assimilation. We grow like who we live with. God's idea of marriage is, *"The two shall become one flesh."* Interestingly, God placed the Law of Oneness within the first institution of life—marriage. Marriage works best when the two work together to become one. (Check out my book *One + One = One: The World's Greatest Love Relationship Equation.)*

This is also a spiritual process. Spend enough time beholding His face, and you will start to look like, act like, and sound like Jesus. **Beholding Him** brings conviction to be like Him. Convictions are the very soul of life. Nothing we do or think is independent of them. Convictions help build our character, influence our behavior, and determine our destiny. Glory brings conviction, and conviction increases desire. The **proof of desire is the pursuit**. All too often, the church gives information about God, but the Kingdom brings conviction as to Who God is.

You can be in a church service without conviction, but you will never have a Kingdom experience without it.

Never settle for information only concerning God and your relationship with Him. **Stay in His Presence until His glory is revealed to you, and you will be transformed into His likeness and His image.**

The universal Law of Transformation helps us to adjust our lives to the one He created us for. Transformation must begin in your spirit.

"So here's what I want you to do, God helping you: Take your ***everyday, ordinary life*** *—your sleeping, eating, going-to-work, and* ***walking-around life*** *—and place it before God as an offering. Embracing what God does for you is the best thing you can do for Him.* ***Don't become so well-adjusted to your culture*** *that you fit into it without thinking. Instead,* ***fix your attention on God***. *You'll be changed from the inside out. Readily recognize what He wants from you, and quickly respond to it. Unlike the culture around you, always dragging you down to its level of immaturity,* ***God brings the best out of you***, *develops well-formed maturity in you" (Romans 12:1-2 MSG).*

Paul is referring to the "covenant life" He calls us to. In prayer, we become one with God. We become one with the person to whom we pray, one with the person with whom we pray, and one with the person for whom we pray. Prayer is always about divine alignment as we move closer to Him and learn to live in Him.

You and I must learn to live and to walk with God. Our experience of receiving Jesus as our Lord and Savior begins our journey with Him, wherein the right choices and decisions transform our behavior. We are to start moving, walking in His laws, His ways—literally toward Him as He orders our steps.

*God made my life complete when I placed
all the pieces before Him.*

When I got my act together, He gave me a fresh start.

Now I'm alert to God's ways; I don't take God for granted.

*Every day I review the ways He works;
I try not to miss a trick.*

I feel put back together, and I'm watching my step.

*God rewrote the text of my life when I opened
the book of my heart to His eyes.*

What a God! His road stretches straight and smooth.

*Every God-direction is road-tested. Everyone
who runs toward Him makes it.*

(Psalm 18:20-24, 30 MSG)

To help us walk out our Kingdom assignment on Earth, He has given the Holy Spirit to guide us. **The first law of guidance is motion.** It is impossible to guide a car until you get it moving. God will guide us into His Presence if we will start moving toward Him.

It is this movement towards Him where we are **led by the Spirit** and **live in the Spirit.** We have only two choices concerning our **walk** on Earth—in the Spirit or in the flesh. The Holy Spirit is with us and in us. He is our **instructor** concerning life in the Kingdom. He is called alongside us to help, comfort, teach, and guide us.

> *"...He will guide you into all the Truth... He will take of what is Mine and will reveal (declare, disclose, transmit) it to you"* *(John 16:13-14 AMPC).*

A life of faith is not optional—it is imperative. Faith is received as we simply believe and practice His Word—His Word enlightens us.

Through His life and Spirit, God shines His light into our lives. The better we know Him, the better we know ourselves—our true God-identity. His Word makes it very clear that we are created for relationships. **Every human being has a "sense of longing for belonging."** Within each of us is a desire to know—Who am I? Why am I? What am I? All of this relates to identity, purpose, and destiny.

No one ever arrives on Earth without a **God-consciousness**. God placed a piece of Himself (eternity) in Adam's genes. I call it a **God-chip,** which is why we can never escape His Presence. Our humanity was created by God Himself, for Himself. He invested His life within us.

We are all children of God and have the choice of becoming His sons and daughters through spiritual birth. He always intended to be the **center** of our lives, involved in our daily living, and direct and guide our paths. Our **environment** is His Kingdom—living fully surrendered to Him. Our **connection** to Him is secured by His Holy Spirit drawing us unto Him. Our **blueprint** for this life is His covenant—it introduces us to Him, reveals Who He is, tells us what He offers, and shows us how He wants to favor us with abundant life. It is the highest potential relationship with the God of the Universe.

Our Constitution for living the Kingdom Life comes from the Red Letter Teachings of Jesus. God chose us in Christ so that we could choose Him. You are chosen, but you must **choose** to be **chosen**.

The process is simple: We are chosen, changed, charged.

"Long before He laid down Earth's foundations, He had us in mind, had settled on us as the focus of His love, to be made whole and holy by His love. Long, long ago He decided to adopt us into his family through Jesus Christ. (What pleasure He took in planning this!) He wanted us to enter into the celebration of His lavish gift-giving by the hand of His beloved Son" (Ephesians 1:4-6 MSG).

In today's church, we often focus on our human needs, wants, and desires—called felt needs. Many subjects are taught to help people live better human lives. God intends for us, in our spirits, to become all that He created us to be. The focus of any church must be on the teachings of Jesus Christ. We must master them and live them out in our world daily. Church should be the school of the Spirit where you become a powerful, spirit-filled being with His knowledge, wisdom, and power. Your very life draws attention to the power of His Kingdom for whole life transformation—spirit, soul, body. We have failed to accomplish our Kingdom mission when we educate our humanity without educating our spirits.

Covenant life is necessary to obtain an authentic, genuine life and fully become Who He made us to be. We become God's family joined together in His love. Those who choose to activate and live in covenant with God become chosen, elected, empowered with great faith, and equipped for great exploits. Individually, we are given a specific mission where God **partners** with us. God elects and chooses based on inclusion—not exclusion. He "wills that all men should be saved and come to the knowledge of the Truth." His covenant brings knowledge and relationship. We become a chosen generation—literally of kings and priests on Earth.

> "And **formed** us into a Kingdom (a royal race), priests to His God and Father – to Him be the glory and the power and the majesty and the dominion throughout the ages and forever and ever. Amen (so be it)" (Revelation 1:6 AMPC).

As His kings on Earth, we decree and declare things as God wants. He lives in us, governs our lives, and fashions our characters as we daily yield to His Lordship. He then imparts abilities, capabilities, energies, spiritual disciplines, and visions to make us efficient instruments of His Kingdom power to those around us.

> "Jesus handed out gifts above and below, filled Heaven with His gifts, filled Earth with His gifts...until we're all moving rhythmically and easily with each other, efficient and graceful in response to God's Son, fully mature adults, fully developed within and without, fully alive like Christ" (Ephesians 4:12-13 MSG).

As His priests, we have **direct access to God, to His Presence**. By this covenant relationship, we become a chosen generation—a royal nation. We are **one Kingdom**, **one constitution** (the Red Letter Teachings), and we have **one government** (a covenant) and form **one great society**.

Our **God-assignment** is to be the solution to all human challenges. Unfortunately, the church, in many ways, has failed to consider the sin of racism. No institution on Earth is better equipped to handle this challenge than a Kingdom-minded church. The unification of the human race is to be accomplished by covenant people who live their covenant identities as His Kingdom spreads throughout Earth. **His holiness is His wholeness.** As the spiritual community grows, expands, and permeates society, a world of order, beauty, and harmony will exist from the chaos of human selfishness, strife, and struggles. Covenant life brings creative faith to surmount and conquer a Godless culture. This requires a peculiar people, God's own personal possession. These are the ones God preserves, treasures up, invests in, pouring into their lives and through their lives His **excellent mercies and perfections**.

Somehow, the church has begun to look too much like the world. Anytime the church loses its Kingdom perspective, its power to influence the culture is greatly diminished. Our national destiny is not determined by Washington DC, the president, Congress, the Supreme Court, politicians, Wall Street, or the educational system. It is determined by God-defined people—those sold out to Him and owned by Him. These Kingdom-minded people, by their daily lives, deeds, words, and actions, continuously build His Kingdom on Earth. They preach by living the Gospel of the Kingdom as Jesus builds His Church. Kingdom-minded people surrender to God's purpose and thus receive God's favor.

Our nation's Founding Fathers believed in, worshiped, and prayed to our God and Savior, Jesus Christ. They wanted, they expected, and they pursued God. The glory of America is, was, and always will be our worship of the only true and living God, Jehovah. Our task today is to **bring back His glory** to our once-glorious nation. Though the formula is more than 3,000 years old, it has always worked and always will.

"...If My people, My God-defined people, respond by **humbling** *themselves,* **praying, seeking My Presence,** *and turning their backs on their wicked lives, I'll be there ready for you: I'll listen from Heaven, forgive their sins, and restore their land to health" (2 Chronicles 7:14 MSG).*

Unfortunately in America, some are often interested in church building rather than Kingdom building. In many cases, some have usurped the authority within the church and ruled by their decrees. In the Kingdom, the Holy Spirit is always the CEO (chief executive officer) and the COO (chief operating officer). God builds His Kingdom through us and uses the church as the agency. This fact is essential to create a continuing unity of vision so that reaching and teaching come from the words of Jesus Himself.

How do we "bring back His **glory** to our nation"? For those of us who serve in full-time ministry (apostles, prophets, evangelists, pastors, teachers), there must be a return to Kingdom building. We must humbly submit our human visions, goals, and desires at the Cross and receive a divine commission to build His Kingdom. Let us return to pursuing Christ instead of man-built, man-led, man-dominated church organizations.

God is, was, and always will be in control of all creation—namely His Kingdom on Earth. As we watch our world on fire with terrorism, hate, anger, rioting, and sexual perversion (transgenderism, same-sex marriage), we must be reminded that He is not caught by surprise, and He is working His plan. He sovereignly controls the Universe and all the inhabitants within.

Why is there such great unrest in the Earth?
Why are people so unaware of life's true meaning?
Why is there so much tension and strife in our homes, marriages, and families?

Perhaps it is because we are unsure of the real meaning of life, our true purpose, and why we are here. Our reason for our existence on planet Earth is to build the Kingdom of our Almighty God and live within that Kingdom's supernatural structure—the **Fourth Dimension. Kingdom worship**—the kind going on around the Throne of God—is what we're missing on Earth. There is nothing more moving, more powerful, more glorious than people genuinely worshiping Him for Who He truly is.

Keys to Activate Your Kingdom Destiny

Chapter 5

🔑 Jesus created His Church as the agency through which His Kingdom is manifested.

🔑 In the church, I learn to become a temple of God.

🔑 The church is always a living organism—not an organization.

🔑 In the Kingdom, I become the physical and spiritual extension of the life of Jesus.

🔑 My Kingdom gifts, talents, and abilities are manifested through the church to enlarge the Kingdom.

🔑 I am a never-ceasing, spiritual being with an eternal calling to participate with God in ruling His Kingdom on Earth.

🔑 I must activate my Kingdom gifts.

🔑 Only through the Kingdom is my spiritual destiny activated.

🔑 The Kingdom is about the education of my spirit.

🔑 In the Kingdom, I experience my God-assigned identity.

🔑 In the Kingdom, God is both my reward and my Rewarder.

🔑 I can be in church without experiencing conviction, but I'll never have a Kingdom experience without it.

Chapter 6

The Kingdom:
Worship Power

OF all the activities of human beings upon the Earth, nothing comes close to matching the activity of Kingdom worship. Worship is focused on Who God is and Who He wants to be in our lives. Worship is powerfully energetic and life-transforming.

> "Christian worship is the most momentous, the most urgent, and the most glorious action that can take place in human life." —Karl Barth, theologian

The fuel of worship is a pure vision of God's greatness. The quickening power of the Holy Spirit is the fire that causes the fuel to burn white-hot. God has never created an inner drive for which He failed to provide a channel of fulfillment.

Worship is referred to over 270 times in some form in the Bible, and it is the central theme. All of His creation is to worship Him.

"Let all the angels of God worship Him" (Hebrews 1:6 AMPC).

In Revelation 4:6-8, John describes the sense of being transported to God's Throne Room—the central site of Heaven.

Awed by its radiant splendor, he describes the living creatures

140

surrounding it as all of them continuously exalt, worship, and adore the Creator. These creatures join the 24 elders to bring glory and honor to God.

More than twenty times, worshiping angels and cherubim are mentioned in the Bible and are always associated with the worship of God at His Throne. More than likely, Lucifer (Satan) was the leader of this order of angels.

The force and flow of these cherubim at worship seem to sweep out from the Throne to the four corners of the Earth (Revelation 5). Every picture of God's Throne shown in the Bible describes His glory and these angelic beings' presence. They are positioned around the Throne at four points in circumference. These living creatures lead and stimulate worship as they draw the attention of all the worshippers on Earth into a chorus unto God.

When you and I worship here on Earth, we join this throng of worshippers around His Throne (Ephesians 3:14-15).

Psalm 22:3 says, God is enthroned upon the praises of His people, and when His Name is hallowed, there is a place prepared for His Kingdom's Throne to "come" and for His will to be done *"on Earth as it is in Heaven" (Matthew 6:9-10).* Our worship of Him brings us into **divine alignment** with the worship around His Throne.

Anyone, anywhere and at any time, who will fully commit themselves to have a Kingdom marriage, a Kingdom family, a Kingdom house, a Kingdom business, or a Kingdom-minded church founded upon pure worship will experience **divine alignment**. One of the most powerful things that John reveals to us is the unity of worship concerning the Kingdom of God. Imagine what would happen if we put aside our denominational and theological differences and simply came to the Cross and the empty tomb to worship Him. Thousands of churches of various denominations, each professing some element of doctrine, have caused great division among themselves. We need the unity of the Spirit and the bond of peace on Earth as we see worship around the Throne. God intended His Church to be one of unity, not division. Only by the power of the Kingdom will unity persist among us.

When we join together in Spirit and in Truth, He will manifest His Presence and His glory. A sustained **posture** of **worship** establishes an alignment in the invisible realm, but in a real and powerful way, places God's Throne "in the midst" of our situation. Any worshiper can make his **house** a center of God's manifested grace and glory. You can only experience God's Kingdom Presence and glory where you live, work, and play when your worship aligns with the worship at His Throne. **Worship brings the entry of God's rule.**

*"When you pray, say, 'Our Father in Heaven,
Holy is Your Name'" (Luke 11:2).*

That is worship. Then we ask for the entry of **God's ruling Presence**—here and now in Kingdom power.

*"Your Kingdom come, Your will be done on Earth as it is in Heaven"
(Matthew 6:10).*

The call to prayer is imperative, active, immediate. The time is now!

It tells us in 2 Corinthians 4:7 that our most natural circumstances will be potential dwelling places for His splendor and glory:

"If you only look at us, you might well miss the brightness. We carry this precious Message around in the unadorned clay pots of our ordinary lives. That's to prevent anyone from confusing God's incomparable power with us" (MSG).

Here is God's glory, ready to be invested in finite and fallible human vessels—**livable spirituality.** We join our worship to the living creatures around His Throne as we experience divine alignment, bringing a manifestation of His Presence here on Earth.

Should you visit a thousand churches during a weekend, you will find many different forms of worship. Some enjoy liturgical, ecclesiastical forms of worship, while others have a more casual yet holy approach to Him. The purpose of worship is always the manifestation of the Kingdom. When His Kingdom is manifested in the midst of us, there are signs, wonders, and miracles—you can expect the supernatural. We need the Presence of the Holy Spirit in the midst of our worship to bring that supernatural element often missing from the dead, dry, ritualistic form of worship.

Worship is love responding to love. Love and worship go like a hand fitting into a **love glove**. Though they are separate, when joined together, they become one. **Love** is the great connector. When we think of God's Throne, it is evident that one is seeing love in action. Love is always connected to true worship. There can never be true Biblical worship without a focus on Godly love. You could say that love is the foundational tenet of worship. It is the most potent medicine to treat the affliction of loneliness and isolation. **Love heals—spiritually, physically, emotionally.**

"Now, because of your obedience to the Truth, you have purified your very souls, and this empowers you to be full of love for your fellow believers. So express this sincere love toward one another passionately and with a pure heart" (1 Peter 1:22 TPT).

As we obey His Truth (Word), our lives are **transformed**, and we practice authentic, passionate expressions of love with pure hearts. A **transformed life** should lead to **transformed relationships**. We are to do this "earnestly" (passionately), which means "at full stretch" or "in an all-out manner, with an intense strain." The word is used to describe a runner who is moving at maximum output with taut muscles straining and stretching to the limit.

"Above all, constantly echo God's intense love for one another, for love will be a canopy over a multitude of sins" (1 Peter 4:8 TPT).

Love covers an offense, sin, hurt, pain—that means it causes something to be hidden, concealed, kept secret, not to be known, or focused on. This Godly love is the greatest virtue of the Christian life—the highest kind of love, a love of the will—**intentional love**. It is the final and fullest expression of spiritual force. Since God is love, there can be no more powerful statement of His nature.

"Endless love beyond measurement that transcends our understanding—this extravagant love pours into you until you are filled to overflowing with the fullness of God!" (Ephesians 3:19 TPT).

When there is this type of expressive love, it leads to authentic worship. Heaven's first priority is worship, which should be the first priority of God's people on Earth. Love the Lord with all your heart, strength, soul, and body is the first thing, and then you worship.

"You can't get second things by putting them first.
You get second things only by putting
first things first." —C.S. Lewis

First things are priorities, non-negotiables you act upon. Priorities begin with the primary purpose of our earthly journey. First of all, you and I exist to know God personally, intimately, exclusively, and worship Him passionately. He created us in love, chose us in love, and planned in love for us to be adopted as His own children (Ephesians 1:4-5).

The focus of your life is revealed in your daily routine. Nothing will ever dominate your life unless you do it daily. Our priorities are revealed in the manner in which we live our lives.

Where do you spend your time?

Where do you spend your money?

What excites you most?

What are you most passionate about?

Our lives reveal a gap between what God expects of us and how we live our daily lives. We have often placed other goals, interests, and joys ahead of the place we should have reserved for the living God. It appears that we love the god of leisure and sports more than we do the living God. Worship at God's house with our families must become a priority—**First Things First**.

"'Go up to the hill country and bring lumber and rebuild [My] house, and I will take pleasure in it and I will be glorified,'" says the Lord "'[by accepting it as done for My glory and by displaying My glory in it]'" (Haggai 1:8 AMPC).

"Take pleasure" means "I will pardon you, favor you, bless you; I will display My glory in you. The heavens will open over you. You will increase, expand, and enlarge your territory. I will satisfy you with My goodness. I will fulfill you with **My Presence**."

First Things First

"But seek (aim at and strive after) first of all His Kingdom and His righteousness (His way of doing and being right), and then all these things taken together will be given you besides" (Matthew 6:33 AMPC).

To "seek first His Kingdom" means to look for, investigate until you find, or strive until you obtain." It embodies the idea of **strenuous effort and activity**. It means to "prioritize not based on our interests, but the interests of the Lord." The Kingdom of God is the **reign of God** in your life. Until you love Him with your whole heart, soul, strength, mind, and body, you will never be ruled by Him.

Is God enthroned in your heart in such a way that **His rule governs your entire life**?

> *"Give God the right to direct your life, and as you trust Him along the way, you'll find He pulled it off perfectly!" (Psalm 37:5 TPT).*

> *"Keep your eyes straight ahead; ignore all sideshow distractions. Watch your step, and the road will stretch out smooth before you. Look neither right nor left; leave evil in the dust" (Proverbs 4:25-27 MSG).*

Keep His Commandments.
Trust His guidance.
Honor His provision.
Accept His instructions.

With His life, suffering, death, and resurrection, Jesus renewed and restored our relationship with God. Our Christian life is designed for worship.

God made us with a need and a desire to worship. True worship is balanced and involves the human spirit, heart, mind, will, and emotions. It requires intelligence but must also reach the depths of our emotional centers and always be motivated by love. It must lead to obedient actions that glorify God. It is personal—always about relationship—and passionate. Worship requires the submission of all our nature to God—spirit, soul, body.

In worship, your spirit is quickened by His Presence as you are made aware of His holiness. Your heart is opened to **His love,** and His Truth nourishes your **mind.** Your will is then surrendered to **His**

will. In obedience to the will of Jesus, your **worship** is in Spirit and in Truth.

We do not worship God for what we get out of it, though it greatly enriches us. Always worship must be Christ-centered, not need-centered. We worship because He is worthy of our worship. We become like the God we worship (image, likeness). We are transformed to become more like Him as we worship Him in Spirit and in Truth.

> *"And all of us, as with unveiled face, [because we] continued to behold [in the Word of God] as in a mirror the glory of the Lord, are constantly being transfigured into His very own image in ever increasing splendor and from one degree of glory to another; [for this comes] from the Lord [Who is] the Spirit"* (2 Corinthians 3:18 AMPC).

Who we are and what we do are both determined by who or what we worship. As a disciple, as goes my worship, so goes my life. Everything I am and do should flow out of the context of worship as the fruit of our communion with Him. **True spiritual worship is a transformational experience.** The entire purpose of God manifesting His Kingdom on Earth is for transformation.

Worship in a Kingdom context will bring about **transformation**, **transition**, and **transference**. It contributes something powerful and lasting to our personalities, relationships, service, and total lives as disciples. Always in true worship, there is a release of energy, which causes **life to be fueled with a higher voltage.**

When we experience and encounter God in worship, we go forth **transformed—stimulated, energized, motivated—**to new levels of exploits in His Name and for His glory. When we go toward the world with its passions and lusts, we are "conformed" and fashion our lives after the pattern of unbelievers.

God wants us to come into His intimate Presence in worship so that He might transform us for our Kingdom assignments. **Always remember there is no Kingdom assignment without divine alignment.**

> *"So will the words that come out of My mouth not come back empty-handed. They'll do the work I sent them to do; they'll complete the assignment I gave them" (Isaiah 55:11 MSG).*

He then desires to transform the lives of the people who are in our world, as well as our circumstances. Those that are transformed are participants, not spectators. In worship, they patiently wait for the Holy Spirit to align them with God's purposes. They produce fruit, not just results. In true worship, God calls us to **wholeness**. He reveals our blemishes and our brokenness to call us into spiritual health. He desires Christlikeness in our character and conduct. He calls us to the "wonder of His Kingdom," "to witness His power," and "to war against our enemy." Let us give Him our Kingdom worship!

Worship will never affect our lives unless it is a daily priority. Often, we have misplaced priorities, which can negatively affect not only our lives but also the lives of those around us. A priority is someone or something of ultimate significance or first in importance.

The question of what life is really about is answered by one simple yet profound word—**glory**. Revealing His glory is the main reason for manifesting His Kingdom on Earth. It is why the heavens exist.

> *"The heavens declare the glory of God..." (Psalm 19:1 AMPC).*

It is why He created us. Moses' cry in the Old Testament simply requested, *"Lord, show us Your glory!"*

> *"Even everyone who is called by My Name, whom I have created for My glory, whom I have formed, whom I have made"*

(Isaiah 43:7 AMPC).

It is why He sent Jesus to Earth.

Jesus said, "I have glorified You down here on the Earth by completing the work that You gave Me to do" (John 17:4 AMPC).

Jesus had one major priority—to bring **glory** to His Father. Our number one focus should also be to **bring glory to His Name**.

God's glory expresses all He is in His being, nature, character, power, and acts. He is glorified when He is allowed to be seen as He really is.

To be where God is is glory.
To be who God intended is glory.
To do what God purposed is glory.

Moses is the only person in the Bible to ask to see God's glory.

"God said, 'I will make my Goodness pass right in front of you...I'll treat well whomever I want to treat well and I'll be kind to whomever I want to be kind.' God continued, 'But you may not see My face. No one can see Me and live.' God said, 'Look, here is a place right beside Me. Put yourself on this rock. When My glory passes by, I'll put you in the cleft of the rock and cover you with My hand until I've passed by. Then I'll take My hand away and you'll see My back. But you won't see My face'" (Exodus 33:19-23 MSG).

Notice what happens when we experience His glory. We see, and we receive His **goodness**. This is God's **benevolence**, His **graciousness**, His **generosity**, His **providence**, and His **provision**.

In Nehemiah 9:25, we see a description of Israel's occupation of the Promised Land: *"And they captured fortified cities and a rich land and took possession of houses full of all good things, cisterns hewn out, vineyards, olive orchards, and fruit trees in abundance. So they ate and were filled and became fat and delighted themselves in Your great goodness" (AMPC).*

Goodness is all that God so generously supplies to make our lives full and complete. He proclaims His Name to us. "Yahweh" means "I Am _____." (You fill in the blank.) "I will be _____." (He will be whatever you need).

People everywhere are feeling empty while searching for meaning, love, direction, and fulfillment. People's emotions are jaded, their minds blinded, their spirits dead, their bodies weakened, and primarily because of wrong or misguided priorities. We desperately need to prioritize our lives to experience an encounter with His glory.

You determine your destiny when you habitually involve yourself in a Kingdom context of worship. Moses had to enter His Presence and linger there for 40 days to fully experience God's glory. Moses realized his great need for God's glory to bring Israel into its destiny.

In worship, God pours the **weight** (glory) of His worth into us to transform our lives.

"And all of us, as with unveiled face, [because we] continued to behold [in the Word of God] as in a mirror the glory of the Lord, are constantly being transfigured into His very own image in ever increasing splendor and from one degree of glory to another..." (2 Corinthians 3:18 AMPC).

Moses was **transformed** by God's **glory**. His anger and discouragement dissipated. When we experience His glory in worship, our unworthiness, inadequacy, insufficiency, emptiness, and neediness are transformed into His goodness. We see Jesus, and through Him, we learn to live in God's glory and experience the practical benefits of the **weight of His glory**.

**That "weight" anchors the soul
when the winds of adversity become fierce.**

**That "weight" will anchor a marriage
in a rocky season and keep it settled in love's commitment.**

**That "weight" will bring a flow of God's provision
into life's daily needs.**

**That "weight" will balance the scales and neutralize the
pain and pressure brought on by life's struggles.**

His glory is transmitted into our beings, bringing **wholeness** into our **incompleteness**, **substance** to life, **love** to relationships, and **truth** to interactions. In essence, it causes us to be our true God-self.

God has adopted us as sons and daughters, which is our destiny, and called us to live a life in which we discover His inheritance in us. **You and I inherit God, and God inherits us**. He reveals our inheritance as we live our Christian life. Paul describes it in Ephesians,

> *"I ask the God of our Master, Jesus Christ, the God of glory—
> to make you intelligent and discerning in knowing Him
> personally, your eyes focused and clear, so that you can see
> exactly what it is He is calling you to do, grasp the immensity
> of this glorious way of life He has for His followers, oh, the
> utter extravagance of His work in us who trust Him—endless
> energy, boundless strength!" (1:17-19 MSG).*

This is the purpose and the effect of seeing the weight of God's glory—to revolutionize the life of every disciple of Jesus. It is entirely possible for every true disciple to see and understand the revelation of God's glory.

> *"And all of us, as with unveiled face, [because we] continued*

to behold [in the Word of God] as in a mirror the glory of the Lord, are constantly being transfigured into His very own image in ever increasing splendor and from one degree of glory to another..." (2 Corinthians 3:18 AMPC).

Once He reveals to you His glory, you'll have an ever-expanding revelation of God in the way He wants to be known by you. Our greatest worship occurs when we lay hold of the rights He has given us in His Word.

Worship, pure worship, equips and empowers us with confidence to become all He says we are—as He pours His nature into us. Real, genuine, authentic worship manifests His glory in which He causes us to be like Him. When He is enthroned within our human spirits, He gains an inheritance in us. Christ is then richer for possessing you, and you are richer for having Him.

"In Him we also were made (God's) heritage (portion) and we obtained an inheritance..." (Ephesians 1:11 AMPC).

You become a beacon of His light to those around you living in darkness. He gains a vessel through which He can heal other wounded souls. He gains an instrument through whom and with whom His grace and mercy flow to hurting and bound people. **He gains whatever He possesses and magnifies that vessel's gifts, talents, and abilities beyond mere human possibility.**

It is Christ in you, your hope of glory—literally, that you experience everything that God is through your human spirit (*Colossians 1:27*).

Christ makes a bold proclamation over us: *"I have given to them the glory and honor which You have given Me, that they may be one [even] as We are one" (John 17:22 AMPC).*

We can receive and enjoy to the fullest measure the glory He has given to us. A life filled with His glory becomes exciting. Even challenges and difficulties are seen as adventures that will stretch and perfect us as He, through us, works everything according to the purpose of His will. Knowing God as He wants to be known to you is the most exhilarating relationship you can experience. It is the secret of a life of fulfillment and energy.

Paul prays for us: *"...that you may be filled [through all your being] unto all the fullness of God [may have the richest measure of the divine Presence, and become a body wholly filled and flooded with God Himself]! Now to Him Who, by (in consequence of) the [action of His] power that is at work within us, is able to [carry out His purpose and] do superabundantly, far over and above all that we [dare] ask or think [infinitely beyond our highest prayers, desires, thoughts, hopes, or dreams]—To Him be glory in the church..."* (Ephesians 3:19-21 AMPC).

The fullest measure of God you will ever experience is through true Biblical worship. Remember, He came and died so He could live in and through you.

We are to know, understand, and practice Christ living in us **now**—Christ in you, the hope of glory.

He came as a human being to **perfect** humanity.

He had to perfect humanity to **redeem** our sinful flesh.

He had to redeem our sinful flesh so that we could **receive** His eternal life.

We must have His eternal life to **live** as He lived.

We must **glorify** Him when He is seen as He truly is in our daily living.

The heart of worship becomes a revitalizing action from the

Spirit of God into our inner being. Worship becomes our greatest weapon and our greatest blessing. Worship is always at the center of God's purpose for humanity. True worship expresses a heart in awe of God's greatness. It is an overflow of a heart hungry for His Presence and in pursuit of His manifested glory.

True, authentic, Christ-centered worship will turn ordinary disciples into radical lovers of Jesus Christ and warriors who accomplish extraordinary exploits for God's Kingdom. Our genuine worship of Jesus will bring a mighty manifestation of God's Kingdom power with signs, wonders, and miracles—supernatural things will happen. In pure heart-felt worship, we begin to see, understand, and enter into the fullness of His Kingdom.

Deep, passionate worship causes **Kingdom-mindedness**. The more Kingdom-minded we become, the less worldly-minded we live. Our worship must become radically **God-centered**. When you desire Him—His Presence, His glory—more than you desire your next breath, you experience true worship. You minimize your earthly challenges and struggles as you magnify Him above all else.

Worship must become our lifestyle.

"No matter what, I will continue to hope and passionately cling to Christ so that He will be openly revealed through me before everyone's eyes. So I will not be ashamed! In my life or in my death, Christ will be magnified in me. My true life is the Anointed One, and dying means gaining more of Him" (Philippians 1:20-21 TPT).

Paul's one goal in life was to "go hard after God." Paul savored Him, treasured Him, and was always satisfied in Him.

Christ was everything to Paul.

"To truly know Him meant letting go of everything from my

past and throwing all my boasting on the garbage heap. It's all like a pile of manure to me now, so that I may be enriched in the reality of knowing Jesus Christ and embrace Him as Lord in all of His greatness. My passion is to be consumed with Him and not cling to my own 'righteousness' based in keeping the written Law. My only 'righteousness' will be His, based on the faithfulness of Jesus Christ—the very righteousness that comes from God" (Philippians 3:8-10 TPT).

Pursuit is proof of desire. When you are satisfied in Him, you stop focusing on what you need from Him. **True worship is all about Who He is.** We don't worship Him to receive from Him but to give Him all of us—spirit, soul, body. Our worship is an end in itself. There could be hundreds of great benefits for us, but that is not the purpose of our worship.

Luke uses a four-fold description of how we are to worship Him—

*"...You must love the Lord your God with all your **heart** and with all your **soul** and with all your **strength** and with all your **mind**..." (Luke 10:27 AMPC).*

As we love Him with all of our **heart, soul, strength,** and **mind, we enter into the realm of His Kingdom on Earth.** Worship like this brings about great exploits which attract the attention of others. Our fully integrated being—spirit, soul, body—is made visible to the world around us in its fullest and most mature form.

> **He desires and covets your attention.**
> **He desires and covets your affection.**
> **He desires and covets your ability.**

In life, it is not necessarily what you do that matters—it is "who" you do it for.

Real purpose-driven living happens daily in ordinary, routine, mundane things.

"So here's what I want you to do, God helping you: Take your everyday, ordinary life—your sleeping, eating, going-to-work, and walking-around life – and place it before God as an offering...fix your attention on God...readily recognize what He wants from you, and quickly respond to it..." (Romans 12:1-2 MSG).

Worship is whatever you are giving your primary attention to, whatever you are giving your primary affection to, whatever you are giving your primary abilities to, and whatever you are giving your primary resources to.

Worship is a lifestyle that God has qualified each of us to live. All of us—warts, sins, failures, shortcomings—can now have free access into His very Presence.

When you and I on Earth worship in Spirit and in Truth with our whole heart, soul, strength, and mind, we join with the throng of worshippers around His Throne in Heaven.

"And since we now have a magnificent High Priest to welcome us into God's House, we come closer to God and approach Him with an open heart, fully convinced that nothing will keep us at a distance from Him. For our hearts have been sprinkled with blood to remove impurity, and we have been freed from an accusing conscience. Now we are clean, unstained, and presentable to God inside and out!" (Hebrews 10:21-22 TPT).

We are to **draw near** in full assurance of faith. We must not bend or yield to the winds of pressure that blow upon us from a seductive and hostile world. At times, we cling to and hold onto our faith, knowing that He Who promised is faithful to deliver. **Hang on—God is on His way with resources for endurance.**

Let us consider one another—observe well or understand one another in a reciprocal relationship of love and acceptance. Knowing one another deeply and intimately creates and releases an attitude of love and earns us the right to poke and push each other. **Worship makes us radioactive for God as we become His radiance in the world.**

Without exception, true worship is a journey into the very Presence and power of God Himself. There, we encounter the awe, reverence, and wonder of Who He is. Worship causes us to transcend our often monotonous, everyday life and to experience His glory and magnificence.

"For God, Who said, 'Let brilliant light shine out of darkness,' is the One Who has cascaded His light into us—the brilliant dawning light of the glorious knowledge of God as we gaze into the face of Jesus Christ" (2 Corinthians 4:6 TPT).

Genuine worship of God enlarges our intellects, expands our souls, and fires our spirits. It is not an escape from our troubled, conflicted, polluted, corrupted environment. Worship is speaking to God about God.

Worship is the submission of our entire being, where we discover the glory of *Psalm 46:1*—*"God is our Refuge and Strength"* (AMPC).

Our consciences are made alive by His holiness.
Our minds are nurtured with His Truth.
Our imaginations are filled with wonder at His majesty.
Our hearts are receptive to His pure love.

He **hides** us so that He might **help** us. We are not refugees looking for an escape—we are wounded and weary pilgrims who need to experience the glory and beauty of His mighty Presence and be refreshed by Him.

You cannot truly worship without experiencing spiritual **enlargement, enrichment,** and **empowerment,** yet that is **not the purpose** of your worship. With every worship encounter, you are **increased in wisdom, knowledge,** and **understanding**—the essence of His being.

> *"Who could ever wrap their minds around the riches of God, the depth of His wisdom, and the marvel of His perfect knowledge? Who could ever explain the wonder of His decisions or search out the mysterious way He carries out His plans?" (Romans 11:33 TPT).*

Worship is a transforming experience. It is our response of all that we are—spirit, soul, body, heart, strength, mind—to all that God is, says, and does. He genuinely desires that everything we are and do shall flow out of worship as **blessed by-products of our oneness with Him.**

Worship always involves **releasing energy**—from us to Him and from Him to us. It is a transforming experience that causes us to live at a higher level, with a **higher voltage.** God always desires that His nature within us shine forth from the inside to the outside.

His disciples got a firsthand view of this on the Mount of Transfiguration.

> *"Then Jesus' appearance was dramatically altered. A radiant light as bright as the sun poured from His face. And His clothing became luminescent – dazzling like lightning. He was transfigured before their very eyes" (Matthew 17:2 TPT).*

The glory of God that was within Jesus radiated outwardly in shadowless splendor. In like manner, He wants to transform us. He wants to work through us to transform the people and circumstances that make up our lives.

In worship, He fills us with **revelation**. As a result, we re-enter our everyday life better equipped, more empowered, and more radiant than before.

> *"I pray that the Father of glory, the God of our Lord Jesus Christ, would impart to you the riches of the Spirit of wisdom and the Spirit of revelation to know Him through your deepening intimacy with Him. I pray that the light of God will illuminate the eyes of your imagination, flooding you with light, until you experience the full revelation of the hope of His calling...that you will continually experience the immeasurable greatness of God's power made available to you through faith. Then your lives will be an advertisement of this immense power as it works through you!" (Ephesians 1:17-19 TPT).*

Worship must not stop with a personal, intimate experience. It must lead to a practical ministry experience—something we do with our lives to help others and honor God. **Living the Fourth Dimension** should radiate His goodness to others. This results in an overwhelming display of His power through you into the lives of those He brings across your path.

There is a truth, a spiritual principle found throughout God's Word concerning His relationship with us:

Life is enriched, empowered, energized, cleansed, and uplifted by the entrance of His life into ours—wisdom, revelation, knowledge, and enlightenment.

Wisdom involves insight, discrimination, choice, and steadfast pursuit.

Revelation means God makes Himself better known to you—He reveals the hidden secrets of His Kingdom (*Psalm 25:14*).

Knowledge is full and complete as opposed to partial and imperfect.

Enlightenment refers to the **eyes of your heart**. You begin to understand the things of God and of His Kingdom.

His purpose is to lead us to our **highest life**. His method for this transformation is true, genuine, real, authentic worship. Worship is God's cure for life's struggles and challenges. Things don't always work out. However, God works out things through a manifestation of the **Fourth Dimension** life into our being.

The solution—

"May He grant you out of the rich treasury of His glory to be strengthened and reinforced with mighty power in the inner man by the [Holy] Spirit [Himself indwelling your innermost being and personality]. May Christ through your faith [actually] dwell (settle down, abide, make His permanent home) in your hearts" (Ephesians 3:16-17 AMPC).

Christ is the glory of God manifested in His Church and within us. **Glory is the majesty and might of God's Presence.**

His Presence in the present is His present to us.

You and I are called to be a Christ-centered fellowship of disciples. Worship is our lifeline to His Presence—our cure, our antidote to life's ills. "Inner man" (or human spirit) is your unseen self in which His Holy Spirit dwells and gives us inner strength: intellect, affections, desires, tastes, conscience, and imagination. It is you being conscious of yourself as a moral personality. It is the real you, the authentic you, the God-you.

In worship, you will be strengthened with a power that fills and floods all of your being, enabling you to withstand any attack and equipping you to serve and to witness for Jesus. Life has a way of immobilizing us. It can sap our energy, drain our courage, and exhaust our patience. However, in the **Fourth Dimension,** those

Kingdom resources of **energy**, **patience**, and **courage** are **renewed**. We need His strength to think clearly and rationally, to love in spite of, and to endure consistently.

His strength fills up our finite reserves with the infinite source of His power.

"And we pray that you would be energized with all His explosive power from the realm of His magnificent glory, filling you with great hope" (Colossians 1:11 TPT).

**Jesus will go before you to show you the way,
behind you to be your rearguard,
beside you to befriend and comfort you,
above you to watch over you,
and within you to give you inner peace and courage.**

Our physical heart is a marvel and a wonder. Each day, it beats 100,000 times. The human heart will beat **more than 2.5 billion times during an average lifetime.** The heart sends 2,000 gallons of blood through our bodies. That blood flows through 60,000 miles of blood vessels, feeding our organs and tissues.

Our spiritual hearts are even more amazing. Its purpose is to receive Christ's Spirit, becoming His **post-resurrection home**! We were born with a physical heart and reborn spiritually with a new heart. **Our worship flows From an enlightened heart filled with God's Truth.** And in that spiritual heart, Christ strengthens us with might to overcome any attempt by the enemy to cause us to lose heart.

Ephesians 3:13 (AMP)– "So I ask you not to lose heart...."

Lose heart can mean **giving in to the forces of evil, misbehaving, being cowardly,** and **losing courage.** Watch what you say and how you react to adversity. Don't become dispirited, downcast, or lose hope. In essence, watch your behavior during challenging times. The enemy always focuses on diverting our attention from the worship of God. Worship is our lifeline in the **Fourth Dimension** of life. As God knows you, you will know yourself. In His **Presence**, there is a continual unveiling of **who** you are, **why** you are, and your Kingdom **purpose**. You have never arrived at your true self because He is ever transforming you.

Within every person, there is a never-ending desire to know and to be known by God. Without worship, man will never understand the Kingdom context of life, which is only found through true worship.

Man is created as a worshipper and may never experience his true being until he worships the One true God, Jehovah, and His Son, Jesus. That experience of worship brings a release to man's spirit, enabling him to live his highest life. God's nature infused into our lives increases exponentially the influence we have on those around us.

In Genesis 1, God invited us to partner with Him, to rule Earth for the glory of His Kingdom and the good of all mankind. Our relationship and rule under God on the Earth are fueled by a **covenant of intimacy** with Him. God has created us to become partners in His **highest Kingdom purposes**. His entire plan of redemption includes restoration of the rule given to Adam in the Garden—dominion, authority, creative responsibility, and accountability.

In Egypt, God delivered Israel out of bondage into worship—because through worshipping Him, they would come to know the heart and nature of the One Who promised *(Exodus 3:12,17)*. God is saying to Moses (and to the children of Israel) that worship is His purpose for them and His key to their destiny. The pathway to His purpose is the pathway of worship. Before the open Red Sea, there was an awaiting mountain (Horeb). They were released so they could go and worship.

We are called to **liberty** and **intimacy** with Him.

"Now therefore, if you will obey My voice in Truth and keep My covenant, then you shall be My own peculiar possession and treasure..." (Exodus 19:5 AMPC).

His objective in liberating them, vanquishing the Egyptians, and bringing them to Sinai is to establish a special relationship: *"I brought you unto Myself...you shall be a special treasure to Me"* (Exodus 19:5).

Their **deliverance**, **purpose**, **destiny**, and **future** were all accomplished by their worship. **Worship** was to be their **lifestyle**, culture, nationality, and religion. What God meant for the Jewish people is what He means for us today. The Covenant of Abraham is now ours.

We are to live a **lifestyle of worship**, creating a **culture of worship** that distinguishes us from the world and marks us as His chosen people. Today, as then, worship brings into our midst a manifestation of Kingdom authority, which will energize our lives and expand our spiritual horizons. Through worship, we bring His Kingdom to Earth. God intended for you and me to experience a manifestation of His Kingdom in the here and now—not just at some future moment.

Keys to Activate Your Kingdom Destiny

Chapter 6

- I am created and qualified for a worship lifestyle.

- My worship must always be Christ-centered.

- My worship brings wholeness into my life.

- The fullest measure of God I will ever experience is through true Biblical worship.

- My worship brings the entry of God's rule into my life.

- Worship must become our lifestyle.

- True worship is all about who He is.

- Worship makes me radioactive for God in my world.

- Genuine worship enlarges my intellect, expands my soul, and fires my spirit.

- My worship is a transformational experience.

- The more Kingdom-minded I am, the more I will be divinely aligned with God's will.

The Kingdom:
Now and Then

**There is healing and wholeness for every
person who chooses a Kingdom life.**

IN the Garden, Adam and Eve experienced original glory before
original sin. They began life as their true, authentic, genuine God-
selves—**they were complete.** God desires that through His Son,
Jesus, **every believer will experience the complete recovery of
spirit, soul, body**—a process that was interrupted by the original
sin in the Garden. Whatever is said about the Kingdom, there is
no question of its intent to bring personal **wholeness** to the entire
human being.

He has commissioned the Holy Spirit to fill our lives with **His
Presence and** heal us from **brokenness.** We are told to be holy as
God is holy. **Holiness** is defined as an attribute of God, the perfection
of Christ's nature, the believer's position in Christ, or the believer's
manner of living. The words **holy** and **holiness** occur some 700
times in the Bible. Holy and holiness are really all about wholeness.
This act of God on our behalf is for this life—something God Himself
will do, and it involves peace, completeness, and wholeness.

The Kingdom age is without end, while the church is only made for this world. Even from the beginning, there was always the thought of a Kingdom. God always considered the establishment of His Kingdom on Earth to give people a foretaste of how the Kingdom operates.

The nation of Israel experienced a revelation of power and authority as they were taken from Egypt to the Promised Land. Throughout thousands of years, God has protected His Kingdom people (Israel) while expanding that Kingdom to include Gentiles.

When Jesus came, His primary mission was to reveal the Kingdom (Mark 1:15—Literal Translation). **Everything** Jesus said and did while He was on Earth was to reveal His Kingdom's authority, power, and anointing. Every miracle He performed was to manifest **the Kingdom.**

When He unstopped deaf ears and opened blinded eyes,
He was revealing the **healing power** of the Kingdom.

When He told Peter to check inside the mouth of the fish,
He was revealing the **provisional power** of the Kingdom.

When He raised Lazarus from the dead,
He was revealing the **resurrection power**
of the Kingdom over death.

Eventually, He would reveal the supreme **power over death** when He raised Himself from the dead.

He intended for His disciples to focus on establishing His Kingdom on Earth. He taught us to *"seek first the Kingdom of God and His righteousness."*

He even taught us to pray,

"Your Kingdom come, Your will be done, on Earth as it is in Heaven" (Matthew 6:10).

His Kingdom manifested on the Earth was His everyday life. However, at the same time, He taught us there was an **eternal manifestation of His Kingdom**—one we would participate in with Him forever. Jesus knew that not everyone who would receive Him as Lord and Savior would become Kingdom disciples. In the Old Testament Tabernacle, there were three different courts—the **outer court**, the **inner court**, and the **Holy of Holies.** In the outer court was the brazen altar where a sacrifice for sin was offered, representing entrance into the Kingdom. The inner court was a place of consecration—"going deeper"—rather than living a shallow Christian life. The third court was the Holy of Holies, where **God showed up with His Presence, power, and authority**. Today, we are permitted to live as Holy of Holies people and to have face-to-face encounters with the living God.

Unfortunately, **many people have a casual relationship with Jesus.** Many churches have failed to teach the concept of the Kingdom here on Earth. When there is a manifestation of the Kingdom, there are always signs, wonders, and miracles—the supernatural is a part of the Kingdom. **One of the reasons for the proliferation of new-age ideologies is the void left by postmodern Christianity, which lacks manifestation of His Kingdom power.**

Postmodernism has become the prevailing mode of thought influencing our culture in the last two or three decades. Postmodernism is a worldview that asserts external and absolute truth cannot be known through reason or science since truth is either nonexistent or unknowable. It says experience is more reliable than reason. For the post-modernist, the idea of truth is created rather than discovered.

For every believer, lingering questions beg an answer throughout life:

What is God's Kingdom will for me?
What truth needs to be discovered in my daily walk with Him?

Paul declares that we are to *"prove (for yourselves) what is the good and acceptable will of God, even the thing which is good and acceptable and perfect (in His sight for you)"* (Romans 12:2 AMPC).

It is asked in moments of great **challenge**, in moments of **opportunity**, in times of **desperation**, and often in times of **distress**. And many times, I've asked myself this question: *How may I come to know His Kingdom will for me?*

The study and pursuit of His will is meant to influence our character and to reshape our lives. Our participation with Him in His Kingdom on Earth helps us transform into Jesus' image and likeness. From the beginning of Creation, God intended for us to **look** like Him, **act** like Him, **speak** like Him. As citizens of Heaven, our loyalty is to our God and King even as we live here on Earth.

Philippians 3:20 (NIV) says, "Our citizenship is in Heaven."

The New Testament has two distinct words for "will."

First, there is His decreed or sovereign will.

Satan, sin, sickness, disease, and death will be judged and rendered powerless forever. Throughout eternity, the Universe—the new Heaven, the new Earth—will be ruled by His sovereign will.

Second, there is His will of desire. This is what God desires to see happen under the best of circumstances.

In Matthew 6:10, we are commanded to pray for God's sovereign will to be *"done on Earth as it is in Heaven."*

We are to pray that God will do as He has purposed to do and accomplish it in and through us. *"Your will be done in me"* is the most difficult prayer to pray sincerely.

Consider:

1. God has a "Kingdom will" concerning each of our lives.

2. His "will" encompasses His Kingdom desires for our lives.

3. You also have a "will" that encompasses your human desire for your life.

4. Those two "wills" are often in conflict with each other (flesh and spirit). One is very limiting; the other is limitless.

5. When you pray sincerely, *"Your will be done,"* you are asking God's will to prevail over your will.

Either God calls the shots, or you call the shots. Either He is your Lord and Master, or you are the lord and master. God wants His will to be done on Earth as it is in Heaven.

He does not accept the way things are going on Earth. He wants Satan's works destroyed and sent His Son and the Holy Spirit to transform our lives. They will equip and empower us to transcend our fleshly limitations as we become our true spiritual selves.

"[But] he who commits sin [who practices evildoing] is of the devil [takes his character from the evil one], for the devil has sinned (violated the divine law) from the beginning. The reason the Son of God was made manifest (visible) was to undo (destroy, loosen, and dissolve) the works the devil [has done]" (1 John 3:8 AMPC).

To pray, "Oh, Lord, Your will be done in my life," brings you into conflict with the **Kingdom of Darkness** but also brings a manifestation of the **Kingdom of Light**. Any conflict with the enemy brings an opportunity for God's Kingdom to be manifested and to bring us into His Presence.

"...Make a decisive dedication of your bodies as a living sacrifice, holy (devoted, consecrated) and well pleasing to God, which is your reasonable (rational, intelligent) service and spiritual worship" (Romans 12:1 AMPC).

His aim is that all of life would become **spiritual worship**. As we are "transformed by the renewing of our minds," we turn all of life into worship. Worship brings us into a personal, covenant relationship with God wherein we receive guidance and direction to live our **highest spiritual lives.**

"What a God! His road stretches straight and smooth. Every God-direction is road-tested. Everyone who runs toward Him makes it" (Psalm 18:30 MSG).

We prove His way is best when we stand at the crossroads of life and make a decision that may seem foolish to others.

This was true for John on the island of Patmos, where he eventually died. And it was true for Paul, who was ultimately executed for his faith. We may not always like His will or even believe it's good, acceptable, and perfect. However, I must fully surrender my life to Him to do as He pleases. His will be done!

Prayer and **preaching**, **faith** and **obedience**, **loyalty** and **perseverance** are means by which **His Kingdom comes**. The message and mission of Jesus Christ completely concern His Kingdom operation on Earth. **It is present now on Earth, and it is in the future New Jerusalem. It is invisible, and it is visible. It is from Heaven, and it operates on Earth. His Kingdom comes into me when I accept and do His will—anywhere, any place, any time.** Hence, we must pray, *"Seek first His Kingdom and His righteousness."*

We respond to His Kingdom as we live by His Red Letter teachings, which form the **Constitution of the Kingdom.** Our prayer is for His reign and rule in our hearts. **The heart of God is His Kingdom, and it must become your heart as well.** Its **domain** is in the hearts, minds, and souls of men and women who subject their entire lives into His hands. To rise to the level of spiritual conquerors, daily proving His will is always best for us, is the purpose of His Kingdom in our hearts.

"Yet through it all, this joyful assurance of the realm of Heaven's Kingdom will be proclaimed all over the world, providing every nation with a demonstration of the reality of God..." (Matthew 24:14 TPT).

When we receive and become dominated by the force and power of His Kingdom, a new dimension of living opens up to us that has limitless possibilities—the **Fourth Dimension.** His life flows through us as we minister the life of Jesus to those who have been wounded, hurt, and beaten down by life. His rule in my life offers a hopeful **plan,** a **promise,** and a **purpose** beyond my wildest imagination. Living the Kingdom Life is very expansive—**I am more, better, and greater as Kingdom life is poured through me to others.**

"Never doubt God's mighty power to work in you and accomplish all this. He will achieve infinitely more than your greatest request, your most unbelievable dream, and exceed your wildest imagination! He will outdo them all, for His miraculous power constantly energizes you" (Ephesians 3:20 TPT).

His Kingdom happens when we respond to the seed of His Word that is revealed to us. My life is a seed that God wants to sow not only into the Kingdom but into the world. As you receive **His Word,** He puts **Truth** into your spirit. Failure to hear and perceive

His Truth means your life is void of His answers and solutions. His Truth brings His government, rule, and reign into our world's issues, challenges, marriages, families, bodies, and finances. His Kingdom happens to us, within us, and then through us. It is not dogma; it is action! When His Kingdom is received into our lives, there will be evidence. He will do things to confirm **His Presence** and **His rule** that transcend our human abilities. It is within my reach, and I can touch it. He wants me to operate in it, to be used by its power to fulfill His Kingdom's purpose in and through me.

Adam's rule and domain was the Earth. He sinned and forfeited his Kingdom position. Jesus, the last Adam, came and gave man back his rule, his domain. We are assigned a realm, an arena, and we are made a trustee of that realm. Adam needed his daily meeting with God to draw the provision from Him to rule the Earth. Jesus didn't come only to give us a ticket to Heaven, but He came to reveal the possibility of living a **God-ruled life** filled with **signs**, **wonders**, and **miracles**. He wants us to respond to His Kingdom's rule by bringing everything in our everyday lives under subjection to His rule.

Anything that our adversary still succeeds at isn't because he has a right to. It is because people believe his lies and fail to seek the Truth. **The adversary has no place in your life, anywhere, anytime.**

"Don't give the slanderous accuser, the Devil, an opportunity to manipulate you!" (Ephesians 4:27 TPT).

Respond to the **Good News of His Kingdom**! Take full advantage of your Kingdom rights and privileges. Reign in life through His Kingdom within you. One word describes the power of God's Kingdom on Earth—**abundance.**

"Jesus then came into Galilee announcing the Good News from

God. 'All the preliminaries have been taken care of,' He said, 'And the rule of God is now accessible to everyone. Review your plans for living and base your life on this remarkable new opportunity'" (Mark 1:15 Literal Translation).

Jesus came declaring this message—"My Kingdom is now here on Earth, and I've come to reveal it to you and to demonstrate to you how it works."

There are two powerful facts concerning how the Kingdom operates:

1. His Kingdom is filled with **unlimited provision**.

2. You and I can have total **favor** with the Ruler of that provision.

You can enjoy success, significance, favor, and protection, have enough and then some, and bless and be generous to those in need.

His purpose was for people to know Him and to learn how to function in the laws governing His Kingdom. One of the most powerful laws of His Kingdom on Earth is the **Law of Consecration**. When you are separated, dedicated, and consecrated unto Him, living a surrendered life, He will cause your path to be prosperous and your life to experience unlimited potential. You must, however, surrender what is in your hand (your authority) in order to receive what is in His hand.

When Joshua and the army of Israel fought Jericho and Ai we see a beautiful illustration of this **principle of surrender: Kingdom blessing is the result of consecration.**

"But the Israelites committed a trespass in regard to the devoted things; for Achan son of Carmi, the son of Zabdi, the son of Zerah, of the tribe of Judah, took some of the things devoted [for destruction]. And the anger of the Lord burned against Israel. Israel has sinned; they have transgressed My covenant

which I commanded them. They have taken some of the things devoted [for destruction]; they have stolen, and lied, and put them among their own baggage. That is why the Israelites could not stand before their enemies, but fled before them; they are accursed and have become devoted [for destruction]. I will cease to be with you unless you destroy the accursed [devoted] things among you" (Joshua 7:1, 11, 12 AMPC).

Consecration is placing your life into His hands as He places His Kingdom into your hands. Paul says your body belongs to God. It is His temple, His residence within us. **Consecrate** means **to keep holy, sacred, separated, dedicated, devoted, and set apart for a holy use.** In the Kingdom, **whose I am is more important than who I am.**

The Kingdom on Earth has a language that consists of God's Word and His Spirit. He communicates the knowledge and wisdom of His Kingdom operation on Earth to us by what He says and what the Holy Spirit does. **Empowered with Kingdom authority,** we then release it with our words into the world around us. **God's Word contains His life; likewise, when we speak His Word, we speak His life.**

In Malachi 3, God sends a scathing word to Israel and to us as well.

He says, "I am God, and I change not." (Literally, I am My Word, and I will fulfill My Word concerning you despite your sins.)

It continues to read:

"You ask, 'But how do we return?' "Begin by being honest. Do honest people rob God? But you rob Me day after day. "You ask, 'How have we robbed You?'

"The tithe and the offering—that's how! And now you're under a curse—the whole lot of you—because you're robbing Me. Bring your full tithe to the Temple treasury so there will be ample provisions in my Temple. Test Me in this and see if I don't open up Heaven itself to you and pour out blessings beyond your wildest dreams" (Malachi 3: 7-10 MSG).

Robbery is the worst form of stealing. **Rob** in Hebrew means "to cover over a goblet, to prevent its contents from being poured out." The total meaning is to **block, obstruct,** or **obscure** God and His **Kingdom provision**—making the manifestation of His Kingdom through us null, void, and of no effect.

You are **blocking** My blessings from being poured out into your life.

You are **obstructing** Me and hindering My provision from being placed in your hands.

You are **obscuring** My abundance from others who cannot witness My goodness to you.

We are to **consecrate** our lives and possessions unto God. The opposite of **consecrate** is **execrate**. **Execrate** is often translated as "cursed" or "accursed," as illustrated in Joshua 6 and 7. To **execrate** something is to be used for a secular purpose that is intended to be used only for a holy purpose. Something consecrated to God's holy use is taken and used for a secular purpose. It then becomes **accursed**—devoted to destruction.

In Joshua 6, God told Israel to take the city of Jericho, burn it, and take what remained—gold, silver, bronze, iron—to the treasury of the Tabernacle. One man, Achan, took a gold bar, a silver piece, and an expensive garment. He stole what was consecrated to God, devoted for holy use, and execrated it for his own use. For forty years in the wilderness, Israel had never lost one soldier in battle.

After the victory at Jericho, Israel went to take the small city of Ai. Only 3,000 men went up, and Israel suffered its first defeat when 36 men died. Joshua fell on his face to seek God to find out why this happened. In essence, Joshua said, would to God we had stayed on the other side of the Jordan with the blessing of **spiritual existence** rather than the abundance of **spiritual conquest.**

God said to Joshua, *"Get up off your face. Why are you accusing Me?"*

"But the Israelites committed a trespass in regard to the devoted things; Achan...took some of the things devoted [for destruction]" (Joshua 7:1 AMPC).

"...Israel has sinned; they have transgressed My covenant... they are accursed... unless you destroy the accursed things among you" (Joshua 7:11-12 AMPC).

Achan, his family, and his possessions are stoned and destroyed.

"And you shall do to Ai and its king as you did to Jericho and its king, except that its spoil and its cattle [this time] you shall take as booty for yourselves" (Joshua 8:2 AMPC).

What is consecrated to Him—your **life,** your **gifts,** your **talents,** your **possessions**—He will multiply and **increase,** taking you above and beyond your physical and mental capabilities. Consecrate your all to Him, and He will give you His all.

In life, we often settle for **spiritual existence** rather than **spiritual conquest.** God did not create us to live on the Earth in the power of His Kingdom to spiritually coexist with a sinful world. He gave us Kingdom authority—the **Fourth Dimension**—in order for us to experience **spiritual conquest.** Spiritual conquest results from God manifesting His Kingdom through our lives daily. Victory becomes a way of life. It is always too soon to give up on our fights with the enemy. Spiritual conquest will never be possible without the **Law of Consecration**—granting to Him your entire being—spirit, soul, body—for His honor and glory while you are here on Earth.

In the Kingdom, the **Fourth Dimension**, God says, "It's My way or no way." Because of the world's appeal, the lust of the flesh, and the pride of life, we often compromise to achieve our dreams. Such is the case of the famous singer Glen Campbell, whose song "Rhinestone Cowboy" became a number-one hit. In this song are these words:

"There's been a load of compromising on the road to my horizon, But I'm gonna be where the lights are shining on me."

He certainly compromised much to "live the dream" in his heart. I'm left to wonder whether his price was eventually worth the cost.

Life often demands that we compromise in order to achieve the dreams in our hearts. Some refer to it as an "art," but when does the **art of compromise** become compromising? Some believe it's a sign of weakness and refuse to compromise their faith, principles, and morals. It has been suggested that it's an agreement between two people to achieve a result both agree is wrong. There is no compromise on how God intends for us to live in this world. The Bible is filled with **moral absolutes** concerning our faith and our behaviors. Instead of compromise, God desires **courage**.

Peter asserts that God is holding back the coming of His Son because He doesn't want anyone to be lost.

Peter says, *"Since everything here today might well be gone tomorrow, do you see how essential it is to live a holy life?" (2 Peter 3:11 MSG).*

"So, my dear friends, since this is what you have to look forward to, do your very best to be found living at your best" *(2 Peter 3:14 MSG).*

Your main **occupation** in this world is to secure your position in the world to come. Peter gave two guiding principles to achieve **No Compromise Living**. We are to **exhibit consecrated and holy behavior with devout and Godly qualities.**

Paul writes to Titus that we are to *"adorn ourselves with the doctrine of God, our Savior in every respect"* *(Titus 2:10).* From this word **adorn**, we get our word **cosmetic**—that which we put on to make ourselves physically attractive. It also means to "embellish or to decorate; to beautify." This word means to "arrange in proper order, fitting or orderly, that which is harmonious." Our **behavior, words, attitudes,** and **actions**, with which we adorn ourselves, **reveal** our relationship with Christ. The Bible teaches us to adorn ourselves with Christ—His beauty, anointing, and power.

"For the Lord takes pleasure in His people; He will beautify the humble with salvation and adorn the wretched with victory" *(Psalm 149:4 AMPC).*

"In a word, what I'm saying is, Grow up. *You're Kingdom subjects. Now live like it. Live out your God-created identity. Live generously and graciously toward others, the way God lives toward you"* *(Matthew 5:48 MSG).*

The essential idea of **peace** is unity, of fragments or separated parts being brought together. This is the idea of **adorning** or **wearing God's doctrine (teaching)**. Your spirit is alive in Christ (made holy). Your soul is restored in mind and emotions (made whole). Your physical body, habits, and conditions can become disciplined and recover back to health. Jesus wants you to become holy—complete in all your being, spirit, soul, body—just as He is holy.

There are two things every believer should know about holiness.

First, your holiness is secured before God by your position in Jesus Christ. You are made **positionally holy** when you receive Jesus as your Lord and Savior. We are given the righteousness of Jesus (adorned with it)—justified, which means "made as if we never sinned."

Second, His Word tells us to live holy lives—practice holiness in **thought** and **conduct**.

"Your new life is not like your old life. Your old birth came from mortal sperm; your new birth comes from God's living Word. Just think...a life conceived by God Himself!" (1 Peter 1:23 MSG).

There is to be no compromise on the road to your **spiritual horizon**. You are going to be where His light is shining on you.

"Arise [from the depression and prostration in which circumstances have kept you—rise to a new life]! Shine (be radiant with the glory of the Lord), for your light has come, and the glory of the Lord has risen upon you!" (Isaiah 60:1 AMPC).

Everything about the Kingdom of God is about **wholeness**—the wholeness of God coming into the wholeness of your being.

Leo Tolstoy wrote a book entitled *What Men Live by and Other Tales*. Within it is a short story entitled "Three Questions." It concerns a King who wants to find the answers to what he considers the **three most essential questions in life:**

1. What is the **best time** to do each thing?

2. Who are the **most important people** to work with?

3. What is the **most important thing** to do at all times?

Many educated men attempted to answer the questions, but all came up with different answers. The King decided to disguise himself and seek the advice of a wise hermit in a nearby village. The hermit was digging in a flower bed, and the King joined him. Twice, the King asked his questions, and after the second time, a man emerged from the woods bleeding from a terrible stomach wound. The King tended to him, and the three stayed the night at the hermit's hut. The next day, the wounded man was better and was grateful for the help he had received. He confessed that he knew who the King was and that the King had executed his brother and seized his property. He had come to kill the King, but the guards wounded him in the stomach. The man pledged allegiance to the King and went on his way. Again, the King asked the wise hermit his questions, and the hermit responded that he had just received his answers.

1. The most critical time is **now**. The present is the only time over which we have power.

2. The most important person is **whoever you are with**.

3. The most important thing is to **do good to the person you are with**.

While we are here as agents of His Kingdom, we are constantly being transformed into who we will be forever. This is vividly portrayed in the story of Simon Peter in 2 Peter 1.

Peter begins this chapter using both his names—Simon Peter. Simon means shifting sand, leafy, unstable, and blowing in the wind. In contrast, Peter means—a stone, rock, stable, sure, like the Rock of Gibraltar. He was Simon but transformed into Peter as he came to a *"full personal knowledge of Him Who called us by and to His own glory and excellence."*

Experiential knowledge of Jesus Christ brings about inner **transformation.** He gives us everything we need for life and

Godliness. We must know Him through experience. We must know what we **believe.** Then **add** to it, **grow** in it, and **increase** it. No life ever becomes great without **focus, dedication,** and **discipline.** As we come to know Him intimately, we experience His divine power. This power is released into every facet of our lives as we believe what His Word says—our work, our families, our marriages, our health, our finances, our communities, our relationships. Everything we need for life and Godliness is given to us in Jesus.

Zoe life—real, genuine life—is how God intended for us to live; we lack no good thing. Zoe life is the **God-kind of life.** Kingdom citizens are not spiritual paupers. We are well-equipped to live as spiritual victors, experiencing spiritual conquest. **Godliness** is a love for God, a love for the things God loves, with an attitude and action consistent with that love. Godliness trumps culture.

> *"We were also given absolutely terrific promises to pass on to you—your tickets to participation in the life of God after you turned your back on a world corrupted by lust" (2 Peter 4 MSG).*

The more you know Him, the more you want to know Him. **You must know in order to grow.** This is transformational knowledge.

The church has been very passive; we are not taking the Kingdom by force. To recapture a commitment to Judeo-Christian principles, we must forcefully embrace the power of His Kingdom here on Earth and declare it through signs, wonders, and miracles. In Scripture, it's clear that people could not refute the miracles of Jesus (or whatever they chose to call Him.) The blinded eyes were open, the deaf ears were unstopped, the dead were raised to life, and the lame walked. Today, we must seize the opportunity to reintroduce our nation and world to His Kingdom power on Earth—**Living the Fourth Dimension.** Not doing this would mean a continual deterioration of morality, the likes of which the world has never seen. If you think the unclean spirits of the sins of this world are bad, wait until you see what's in the perverted minds of the sinful. (Homosexual marriage and transgenderism are just the beginning of the perversion that is coming.)

Paul said the whole creation is yearning for the day when God's true sons and daughters will be revealed on Earth. We should never accept mediocrity and the limited human nature life that the vast majority of people on Earth live. When we submit to His Kingdom and its laws, we are far more than what we have become. **It is then that signs, wonders, and miracles attract the unbeliever's attention since the Kingdom of God is supernatural.**

We must embrace and grasp the concept of the **now Kingdom** as well as an eternal one. **It will transform our lives.**

Keys to Activate Your Kingdom Destiny

Chapter 7

- His Kingdom is manifested now to bring wholeness into my life.

- His Kingdom is invisible and visible; it is from Heaven and operates on Earth.

- God's heart is His Kingdom, manifested on Earth. It must become my heart as well.

- Kingdom life poured into me makes me more, better, and greater than I am.

- His Kingdom is filled with unlimited provision, and I have favor with the Ruler of that provision.

- In the Kingdom, whose I am is more important than who I am.

- The Kingdom on Earth is about spiritual conquest, not spiritual existence.

Chapter 8

The Kingdom Mission:
Take It by Force

"God! Arise with awesome power,
and every one of your enemies will scatter
in fear!" (Psalm 68:1 TPT).

FROM the very beginning of mankind, we see a God of action. He is creating, commanding, sustaining, and raising up an army of sons and daughters to do exploits beyond their wildest imagination. Buried inside your human spirit, inside your hard drive, is His plan for your highest life. However, it's not just a gift from God—you must take it by force.

"And from the days of John the Baptist until the present time, the Kingdom of Heaven has endured violent assault, and violent men seize it by force [as a precious prize—a share in the heavenly Kingdom is sought with most ardent zeal and intense exertion]" (Matthew 11:12 AMPC).

What exactly does that mean? **It means the Kingdom is valued, sought after, actionable, progressive, radical, and powerful—something this world has never before seen.** It means that the Kingdom came with such force (Jesus) that it overwhelmed sin, sickness, and disease. People came from everywhere to get in on its benefits. They radically, powerfully seized the Message of the Kingdom.

In the beginning, God intended to reveal how His Kingdom works through a nation of people called the Israelites. He wanted to be their God, their King, in order to display His goodness, generosity, mercy, and love through them. So, the **Kingdom mentality** has existed throughout the history of man.

From the time of the Creation of man in the Garden of Eden until this very moment, it is evident that God has two intentions for the Universe:

- To create a Universe in which man could live and be continuously challenged to explore it

- To introduce into it the laws of His Kingdom

However, it was not until Jesus came that we saw the purest manifestation of what His Kingdom was like. Everything Jesus said and did was about the Kingdom. He begins to show us the power of the Kingdom after forty days of prayer and fasting in the wilderness. Coming out of that experience, He begins a ministry of miracles, signs, and wonders the world has never seen. He showed that everything on the Earth was subject to His power. He opened blinded eyes, unstopped deaf ears, made the lame to walk, caused a miraculous catch of fish, and showed money in a fish's mouth in an effort to reveal to us that the Kingdom is all-sufficient for the needs of mankind. It was as if Jesus told His disciples—watch me operate, and you will see the glory and power of my Father's Kingdom here on the Earth. He says, "*I have come to impart to you, to deposit within you a Kingdom.*" When we see the Red Letter Teachings—the actual words of Jesus—we view the **Constitution of the Kingdom**.

Whether or not someone believes in God, Jesus, or the Bible, you can not possibly live a better life than being obedient to those Teachings. It seems as if He covered what mankind would be confronted with—all the while revealing God's Kingdom on Earth. Many years after His ascension, His disciples and followers continued to operate in the power of the Kingdom. **In so doing, they knew no limitations or boundaries to their accomplishments.**

However, man began to find ways to institutionalize the Message of the Kingdom. Soon the Kingdom was relegated to the agency of the church, and the church began to be run by man, and often, they did not understand the Laws of the Kingdom. As the centuries began to pile one on another, men, religious men, and religious organizations lost sight of His pristine beauty. Isaiah spoke of this Kingdom and its government when he said, *"Of the increase, there will be no end"* (*Isaiah 9:7*). Today, we live in a world that rarely sees the fruit of the Kingdom being manifested through the servants of the Word. Rules, regulations, and denominational beliefs have severely limited the effects of the Kingdom on Earth.

The Holy Spirit was always intended to be the COO and the CEO of God's Kingdom. Through the power and unction, gifts and fruit of the Spirit, mankind would view a **spiritual manifestation** much like in the days when Jesus walked on the Earth. His Kingdom cannot be limited in its scope or power by anything or anyone. Governments today, especially in this nation, have thrown God out of our educational institutions and our government, and they have tried to create a world where God doesn't exist. God mocks their futile attempts to diminish Him or dismiss Him by constantly invading history with a sovereign move of His Presence. He ignores man's laws, rules, and regulations that try to deny His existence and His power in people's lives.

As history reveals, man boxes himself into a corner by godless anti-Christ decisions such as immorality, corruption, and debauchery, along with perversions of all kinds. Suddenly, God breaks into our world and begins to manifest His Presence in the lives of individual people, such as the revivals we witnessed over a short time in America. In 2023, we saw a move of God's Spirit on several college campuses where people gathered informally to witness a fresh manifestation of God's Kingdom. They came from all walks of life and denominational baggage and experienced a fresh outpouring of the Holy Spirit, which revived the Message of the Kingdom of God for man on Earth. No government, no government official, and no religious institution can ever stop the move of His Kingdom. **The Kingdom is. Period!**

Eventually, mankind will learn that while he may control the church, he will never control the Kingdom. All you can do is embrace it and prepare for the wildest spiritual ride you've ever experienced.

But Kingdom living is not just handed to us on a silver platter. There is a war to be fought so that we become the righteousness of God in Jesus Christ. The greatest weapon of **spiritual warfare** is a **righteous life**. Paul said, *"The Kingdom of God is not meat and drink, but righteousness, peace, and joy in the Holy Spirit"* (Romans 14:17). Notice the sequence—it is the righteousness of God that produces peace, which then brings a life of joy from the Lord, as the Nehemiah said, *"The joy of the Lord is our strength"* (verse 8:10 NIV). **Kingdom Living** is more than being a conqueror. It is more than being an overcomer. It's **above and beyond**—the very highest possible human life.

Living the Fourth Dimension requires questions and choices:

- Will you live as a Kingdom citizen or a cultural victim?
- Will you live as a thermometer and reflect the culture around you or as a thermostat impacting and influencing that culture?

- Does your lifestyle line up with your beliefs?

- From where do you get your identity and your values?

- Do you just fit in, or do you stand out?

- Do you live from the outside in or from the inside out?

Living a **counter-cultural lifestyle** is a costly endeavor. There is no question that Christian values, morals, and faith are under attack in America.

Culture is designed not to inform you but to conform you. Slowly but surely, our culture is being transformed with subtle messaging from Hollywood media, governmental, religious, and educational leaders concerning abortion, same-sex marriage, the sanctity of marriage, immorality, sexual perversion, transgenderism, pedophilia, and personal responsibility.

We are witnessing the dawn of the persecuted church in our nation.

In the Kingdom, compromise leads to conformity, which leads to defeat. **What you come to believe determines your behavior. All behavior is need-motivated.** This cultural indoctrination is intended to move you away from strictly held principles of faith, truth, and belief in God.

*"Do not be **conformed** to this world (this age), [fashioned after and adapted to its external, superficial customs], but be transformed (changed) by the [entire] renewal of your mind [by its new ideals and its new attitude], so that you may prove [for yourselves] what is the good and acceptable and perfect will of God, even the thing which is good and acceptable and perfect [in His sight for you]" (Romans 12:2 AMPC).*

God expects and demands that we not allow the culture to fashion or conform us. The word **conform** means **schemed-together-with.**

We get our word **scheme** from the root of it. As believers, we must speak with a prophetic voice in challenging anti-God, anti-Christian messages and messengers, and also simultaneously portray an evangelistic heart of love and acceptance of the person. Our goal as believers in a hostile culture is to ***be transformed by the entire renewal of our minds***.

This transformation is a process. We **transcend our form** to become something better, something more.

God says, "Let us **form** man in our image."
Satan says, "I will **deform** man by sin."
The world says, "We will **conform** man in our image."
Education says, "It will **inform** man with knowledge."
Society says, "We will **reform** man by culture."
Christ says, "I will **transform** man by grace."

We are transformed as we constantly renew our minds with God's Truth. More important than what I "feel" and what I "do" is who I "believe."

In facing the incessant demand of culture to be "inclusive," "progressive," "socialistic," "woke," and "open," we must ask two questions:

What does God's Word say?
What is the righteous thing to do?

Transcending culture spiritually is not the easiest or most popular choice but the most rewarding one. When we **transcend culture**, we rule as Kingdom citizens, something beyond who, where, and what we are.

Without question, Jesus came into this world to introduce to all mankind the power of living as Kingdom citizens while living on Earth among various cultural forces.

What does this mean for you and me today as Kingdom citizens living **Living the Fourth Dimension Life?**

The Kingdom comes with power; it is sovereign, has laws, transforms, heals, delivers, saves, and returns man to his original dominion over God's creation. His rule is now in every spirit-filled believer, continuously transforming and expanding that rule through us to the environment around us. It is a process in which we yield our lives—our gifts, abilities, capabilities, energy, time, and resources—surrendering our all for His glory to be manifested to, within, and through us.

Daily, we are confronted with two significant challenges:

the **mystery of life** and the **mastery of life**

In prayer, we commune with God, Who gives us light to illuminate the mystery and power to become masterful in our living. His power strengthens us within our innermost being.

God intends your human spirit to be the spiritual control room of your soul/body life. You must live with spirit consciousness, always being spirit-filled and spirit-controlled. Then spiritual power is released from within—wisdom, knowledge, and understanding fill your daily life. Your strength to endure life's struggles, understanding to face life's challenges, and power to overcome adversity come from your inner being. Your human spirit must be **clothed** with God's Word, His Spirit, and the fruit of His Spirit to become bold and to speak with authority the message of His Kingdom. **The eyes of your heart give you vertical vision, which is the secret of horizontal endurance.** Live from the inside to the outside; live from your inward, nonphysical, spiritual self, the spirit-supported self, knowing your life is hidden with Christ in God. Wear and tear on the outside, constant renewal on the inside.

Discover the real you—the inner man!

Then you go forth, empowered by His Spirit, to **take His Kingdom by force**.

The message is clear—**total reliance upon God is the doorway into the Kingdom of God—His rule, His reign, His governing power in your daily living**. All you need to exercise your rule in your realm of life has been given to you by the King of the Universe, providing everything you need for life and Godliness (*2 Peter 1:3*).

- I can learn how to **rule** in my life by my behavior, choices, and decisions.

- I do not **yield** to my lusts as I rule my mind, will, and emotions.

- Using His Word as a **guideline**, I will rule in my family, in my marriage, and over my children.

- I come into **Kingdom alignment** with my resources and rule over my daily life, which is lived in a covenant context with God.

Lifestyle and worship are inseparable. Each person worships someone or something. It is in worship that we begin to understand **Living the Fourth Dimension**, which requires a thorough knowledge of Who God is and who we are in Him. We must mesh our lives with God, who meshes His life into us. We are more than our humanity—**we are spiritual beings**. Combining those two entities gives us the resources and power to carry out the Kingdom's cultural mandate on Earth.

Adam learned about life from God, and through the process, he learned about God. Adam and God **walked together as covenant friends. Walking** speaks of action and activity. It defines the entirety of the activities of each life.

Made in God's image and after his likeness, Adam was a full-grown male, a true God-man. His intention was for Adam to continue his human, fleshy growth in daily meetings in which God poured His life into him. **Image and likeness** were intended not just for Adam but also for us. Though he was created in a perfect state, Adam's potential had to be unlocked and experienced as he manifested it in his daily life. The message is simple: **Adam was far more than he had become.** There was a whole world beyond him—more than him, greater than him. God spoke into his life daily as Adam discovered his true God-identity.

First, he had to discover his humanity—gifts, talents, abilities, capabilities, resources, energy, emotions—and then discover his **inner spiritual self (his human spirit).** Not only do we discover our human capabilities, but how they are expanded and enlarged when He blends His life with our humanity. Whatever inherent power is within us, it becomes so much more when God joins the power, glory, and provision of His Kingdom to our lives. It's our human lives on spiritual steroids.

It is always God's intention for us to be **fully actualized, fully alive.** As this begins to take place, we can answer the questions:

Who am I? (identity)
Why am I? (purpose)
What am I? (discovering gifts, talents, abilities)

I don't think anyone wakes up on any given day believing he is adequate for the **cultural mandate** of governing the Earth. But God has granted us the **power of attorney** to use His authority and resources to manifest His Kingdom power on Earth. His resources (power of His Word and the Holy Spirit) provide us with His wisdom, knowledge, and understanding to help others experience their **God-designed lives**. When God made Adam a living being, He simply caused His breath (His life) to flow into Adam. The same is true of us today. By the very breath of His Spirit, we become alive *(1 Corinthians 15:45)*.

> *"And having said this, He breathed on them and said to them, 'Receive the Holy Spirit!'" (John 20:22 AMPC)*.

Thus, our fully alive, highest lives are a combination of the relatively little power residing in our bodies (mind, will, emotions) with the **power inherent in the infinite rule of God's Kingdom**. In essence, God takes everything we are, the person He created us to be, and meshes His life and Kingdom resources into ours. Everything that I am at that moment begins to grow, multiply, increase, enlarge, expand. **Your Kingdom self is limitless**. You are in the world, but you are not of the world. Your everyday walking around-sleeping-eating life becomes supercharged because it's no longer just you. Now, the living God of the Universe, the **omnipresent, omnipotent, omniscient** One, is fully engaged through you as you release Him through deeds, words, and actions—you become the spiritual you on spiritual steroids.

So the Bible defines you as more than a conqueror, more than an overcomer. You have now moved beyond your **human existence** into **spiritual conquest**.

When we walk in covenant with Him, we recover our lost lives, experience deliverance from the curse of sin, and enjoy His Presence. We learn we are not *"our own handiwork,"* and our lives are not our products. We are His; only He knows why and for what He created us. We must take hold of the fact that we are a **product of God**. Our **spiritual walks** are not limited to certain devotional activities such as Bible study, worship, church, etc. They consist of receiving power from His Holy Spirit to become who He had in mind when you were formed in your mother's womb. As we **walk with Him,** He infuses us with His life, creating divine energy within us to produce Godly living through us. **This walk with Him helps you to understand He designed and redesigned you to be the real God-you.** He wants you to become the **highest version** of yourself using all your resources of strength and power for daily living, which are found in His covenant with us.

When our service lines up with His covenant, our walk lines up with His principles, and the world sees Him in our living, we become **full-valued coins** for Him to spend for His Kingdom on Earth.

> *"(Paul prays) That you may walk (live and conduct yourselves) in a manner worthy of the Lord, fully pleasing to Him and desiring to please Him in all things, bearing fruit in every good work and steadily growing and increasing in and by the knowledge of God [with fuller, deeper, and clearer insight, acquaintance, and recognition]. [We pray] that you may be invigorated and strengthened with all power according to the might of His glory, [to exercise] every kind of endurance and patience (perseverance and forbearance) with joy"* (Colossians 1:10-11 AMPC).

Remember that **God has prepared works for us to do,** which can only be accomplished as we *"take the paths which He prepared ahead of time that we should walk in them"* (Ephesians 2:10). Notice why this is necessary: Living the good life which He prearranged and made ready for us to live.

All too often, the church has adapted the world's methods and programs and learned to live without **God's Presence. Many believers long for an experience**—happiness, contentment, security, success, position—and find themselves looking for that rather than an intimate, personal, covenant relationship with God.

A covenant walk guarantees His Presence with us. God wants to do life with us. He offers us **His personalized Presence**—the felt, revealed, personal Presence. Let's remember that God's first communication with man (Adam) was not with words but His Presence (*Genesis 2*). This means God turns His face toward us in favor and acceptance. It means **filling up, pervading, permeating, overspreading, and being in the face of**. It also means to be sufficient, to be able to sustain, or support. He sustains and supports those who walk in covenant with Him; He energizes them. He wants to walk with you in covenant, live through you, and breathe through you so that those around you see God in your living.

As a believer, you are part of Christ—part of God Himself—and **your joy is firmly anchored in becoming who you are—His image, His likeness**.

This enables the One Who created you to be Who He is in you and allows you to be who you are in Him. The questions become for those who desire Kingdom living—**Living the Fourth Dimension:**

What has happened to that kind of life?
Where is the life that we have lost in the living?

To live our true God-life, we must receive, with open arms, **His uncreated life** flowing into **our created life**. This requires us to live a surrendered life, an *exchanged life*, and a trusting life. Our created life was never meant to be fueled by the world around us. We often depend on the people around us for our self-worth and self-esteem. If someone praises us or affirms us, we feel we're valuable. If someone criticizes us, we face a crisis of self-worth. To keep the approval coming and evade the critics, we become **performance-oriented**, trying to please everyone.

Instead of becoming creative, spontaneous, original individuals, we turn into robots just going through the motions without joy, peace, productivity, and fulfillment. God wants you to know that you're part of Someone bigger, greater than you. We are His body and are sustained by His life and His energy. You and I in Christ reconcile the chaotic world to God. He accomplishes this through us as we live in the **Fourth Dimension**—the Kingdom lifestyle. We are in Him, and He is in us. (The phrase *"In Him"* or *"In Christ"* is used over 160 times throughout the Bible.) *"We are a chosen race, a royal priesthood, a dedicated nation, [God's] own purchased, special people" (1 Peter 2:9 AMPC).* We are **God-possessed, God-owned, God-controlled.**

He is building His Kingdom with each of us. Our lives become **living temples.** Our countenance shows forth His love. Our voices speak out about Who He has made us to be. We proclaim His excellencies. We are **living advertisements** of God's goodness, favor, miraculous deeds, and mighty acts.

George Frederic Watts was a famous artist who spent his whole life trying to catch the unseen and put it on canvas for our profit and edification. He painted a great picture called **"The All-Pervading."**

It is a rendering of a magnificent figure with a marvelously spiritual face, the two large wings encircling all things, and it holds the Universe as a globe in its hands. Very impressively, it brings home the fact that underneath the world and all its parts are the everlasting hands, and above and around are the encircling wings of God. The artist's favorite blue background has a strange depth and intensity, which suggests and represents infinity. Watt's painting is trying to teach the solemn truth that God is the **great reality at the core of all things**.

One of the loftiest and most inspiring thoughts of human life is that all the unborn and born things of life that are to create the future are living in their perfect ideas in Him. In that sense, abortion is the murdering of the future—one which God ordained.

"Your eyes saw my unformed substance, and in Your book all the days [of my life] were written before ever they took shape, when as yet there was none of them" (Psalm 139:16 AMPC).

Today begins a baby's life. What about the future of that life—the baby's profession, occupation, purpose, and destiny? And when that child is 40 or 50 years old, his real-life question will be—what?

It's future **unseen**.
It's lessons **unlearned**.
It's discoveries **unmade**.
It's growth **ungrown**.

But in the heart of God, there is a picture of that child's life, what that child may become in the completeness of his life. The real question: How far has he been able to translate into the visible and tangible realities of life that idea in God's mind before he was conceived?

Are you living according to the **heavenly pattern**?
Are you living the life you were created for?

As we live according to His plan and will, His favor flows through us, increasing our **Kingdom value**. Our lives are to be balanced—spirit, soul, body—harmonious, symmetrical. The world should marvel as it looks on us while we are **Living the Fourth Dimension**.

Jesus has given us the best life strategy the world has ever seen, as He lived among us in a tent of flesh.

Jesus became the highest and best example of how to live life. His manner of living, interacting with others, showing a heart of compassion, and being totally obedient to His heavenly Father are obvious marks of genius.

**Genius has been described as the ability
to understand that which is obvious.**

Jesus came into our world to make known to all an invitation to experience a pilgrimage into the life and heart of God. On this journey, we are becoming who we will be—forever. God desires us to learn to live in Him. Jesus' life and words came in the form of information and truth designed to cause a transformation in every life that embraced them. He lived on Earth as the "Prince of Life," dispensing *"abundant life"* through His *"inexhaustible riches"* as the *"Lord of Glory."* Jesus offers Himself as the doorway into this amazing life strategy.

> *"These words I speak to you are not incidental additions to your life, homeowner improvements to your standard of living. They are foundational words, words to build a life on. If you work these words into your life, you are like a smart carpenter who built his house on solid rock. Rain poured down, the river flooded, a tornado hit—but nothing moved that house. It was fixed to the rock" (Matthew 7:24-25 MSG).*

God's creation covenant with humanity indicates He assigned to us collectively the rule over all living things on the Earth – animal and plant. That makes His Kingdom subjects responsible before God for life on Earth—we are equipped for this task by God, Who framed our nature to function in a conscious, personal, intimate relationship of interactive responsibility with Him. We are designed and assigned to exercise our rule only in union with Him as He lives His life through us. When we submit who we are, why we are, and what we are to God, our rule then increases.

As Kingdom people—praying daily, *"Your Kingdom come, Your will be done"*—we are to move out into everyday life as common people who become naturally supernatural—available to the Holy Spirit's direction and anointing. He wants us to manifest in our words, deeds, and actions the power of His Kingdom, which will then draw people to Him.

Speak the Gospel to the poor.

Speak liberty to captive souls.

Heal the sick—**bind up** broken hearts.

Visit the afflicted, imprisoned, and bedridden.

Offer cooling water to thirsty lips and **restore sight** to the blind.

Confront and usurp the control of
entrenched demon powers (Luke 4).

Believe that the same Spirit that raised Jesus from the
dead can manifest His power in lives (Romans 8:11).

Everyone who accepts God's Kingdom rule into their life is born of the same Spirit as Jesus and empowered by the same Spirit Who empowered Him. This causes us to be equipped to share His life, His love, and His power in each situation the Holy Spirit provides for us. We are to go into our everyday life and world and simply **let Jesus happen** through us.

**Life is not about what happens to us
but what happens within us.**

He is not asking for super spirituality, spiritual perfection, or superficial Godliness. Step into any and all situations that confront you and expect God to help you become **naturally supernatural**.

That is living the Glory of His Kingdom in everyday life. **Glory is God's promise** available to any person, family, or group who will align with His divine order. When we praise God despite Satan's attacks, we open the doors of our house to be filled with His glory.

Full-hearted, Biblically-based, Holy Spirit-ignited worship produces His glory in our midst. His glory becomes the increasing portion of anyone who pursues a life of humility before His Throne.

Worshipers live in His Presence and abide in the protection of

His glory. To maintain this glory in our house, we must honor it and Him. He must be the one you turn to, trust in, rely upon, and refuse to doubt.

Glory demands we stay **plugged in** with fresh, vibrant, energetic, whole-hearted worship. When our worship is habitual, ritualized, and shallow, it causes His glory to fade. Our worship must constantly be like a new spring season, with the air filled with the fragrance of fresh blossoms. **Every kingdom must be founded upon basic principles and laws.** It must breed trust in order to govern. His Kingdom is founded upon His Truth, which births trust. Trust is a necessity to our Christian faith and is also one of the foundational laws of His Kingdom.

A trust issue occurred in my own life in ministry. My soul cried out to God for an answer to my huge challenge. He prompted my spirit with this question:

"Do you trust Me?"

Obviously, I replied, "You know I trust You."

He said, "You intellectually trust Me, but
you do not live as if you do."

"Lean on, trust in, and be confident in the Lord with all your heart and mind and do not rely on your own insight or understanding. In all your ways know, recognize, and acknowledge Him, and He will direct and make straight and plain your paths" (Proverbs 3:5-6 AMPC).

No one will question that this is the day of **information overload.** Education and learning have become idols to which many people frequently bow. It is a time of exceeding pride in human knowledge and achievement. We are surrounded by a culture where the desires and rights of the individual are considered sacred—I may have whatever I want or be whomever I will be. It is also a time when trust is on the decline. We live in a highly skeptical society.

How did we get here? We stopped **valuing truth.**

Truth and trust go together—**truth is the foundation of trust.** God created us as persons of trust. We each have the capacity to trust so that we can trust Him and learn to trust each other. Though, at times, it seems like our world is out of control, God is working out His plan and purpose in and through our lives. I can trust Him because He is in control.

"Give God the right to direct your life, and as you trust Him along the way, you'll find He pulled it off perfectly!" (Psalm 37:5 TPT).

Trust is a never-ending process in our earthly journey of faith. Only through a life of trusting God can we live our highest life. Our trust in Him must be complete—**trust is a foundational law of His Kingdom.**

Trust means **being secure without fear, confiding in, and clinging to safety.**

Black's Law Dictionary definition: "A right of property, real or personal, held by one party for the benefit of another. Something that is transferred to someone with the intention that it be administered by a trustee for another's benefit."

God, Who is the sole owner and grantor of everything, makes a deposit into my trust account, and the possessions (gifts, talents, abilities, treasure, etc.) are then managed by me for His Kingdom's sake. He has given us the Gospel of His Kingdom to herald forth to everyone everywhere. Having thus received these blessings and possessions, I must use them to benefit His Kingdom as a trustee. As I sow into others, He pours more into me.

The multiplication begins as I give out to others. God is always eagerly waiting to deposit into my trust account (my spirit) more **capital** to give out to those in my world.

> *"This generous God Who supplies abundant seed for the farmer, which becomes bread for our meals, is even more extravagant toward you. First, He supplies every need, plus more. Then He multiplies the seed as you sow it, so that the harvest of your generosity will grow. You will be abundantly enriched in every way as you give generously on every occasion, for when we take your gifts to those in need, it causes many to give thanks to God" (2 Corinthians 9:10-11 TPT).*

You and I determine our **spiritual blessings** as we trust God's Word, obey it, and watch as He entrusts us with more and more. This requires complete trust in Him, His Word, His promises, and His covenant. Lean on, trust in, and be confident in the Lord with all your heart. We must trust His guidance. Choices, decisions, motives, and intentions must all be directed to what God wants and desires to do through us. We **invest our lives** in **God's Truth and wisdom**.

We are "all in," and we go "all out" for His Kingdom glory. Leaning on "our own understanding" is never an option. We must not trust our motives or our emotions, which are driven by our fleshly desires.

The word **understanding** is used by the wise man Solomon some 54 times in Proverbs. It is the ability to look to the heart of an issue to discern the differences at stake in the choices being weighed. It is closely aligned with wisdom.

> *"Understanding is a wellspring of life to those who have it..."* *(Proverbs 16:22 AMPC).*

Our trust in God leads to a relationship.

> *"Acknowledge Him, recognize Him, know Him, in all your ways..." (Proverbs 3:5).*

This personal bonding from trusting Him results in changes in behavior—we experience a sense of awe, intimacy, and belonging. We do His bidding virtually without having to be reminded. The path we walk is marked out by Him (directed), and the power to walk it is His gift to us—He entrusts us!

Words are powerful.

"Your words are so powerful that they will kill or give life, and the talkative person will reap the consequences" (Proverbs 18:21 TPT).

"A word fitly spoken and in due season is like apples of gold in settings of silver" (Proverbs 25:11 AMPC).

Trust is a powerfully positive word. More than 180 times, the Bible speaks of trust. It is an action word that, when exercised, causes our worries, anxieties, stress, fears, and doubts to be wholly transformed into peace and rest. His Word is geared toward **function and purpose** as it applies to life.

"So trust in the Lord (commit yourself to Him, lean on Him, hope confidently in Him) forever; for the Lord God is an everlasting Rock [the Rock of Ages]" (Isaiah 26:4 AMPC).

When our lives are saturated with God's Word, we have the capacity to operate from a **divine viewpoint** rather than just a **human viewpoint**. When our **human knowledge** is inadequate or in conflict with His Word, it must yield to **divine revelation**. A worldly viewpoint often skews our human reasoning and understanding; therefore, we must grasp **God's perspective** of any situation. We do that through proper understanding and knowledge.

In Proverbs 3:5-6, **"understanding"** is the ability to distinguish the real from the unreal, the true from the false; an ability to observe, gain insight, and then discern to devise a plan or make a decision; to discern the processes of building something.

Acknowledge is not just an academic knowledge of God's Word but an **experiential knowledge** you gain by applying the **Truth of Scripture**. This is an intentional act, a choice, **to be doers of His Word and not merely hearers.**

"Don't assume that you know it all. Run to GOD! Run from evil! Your body will glow with health, your very bones will vibrate with life!" (Proverbs 3:7-8 MSG).

Trust is healing throughout your entire being. Trust brings total, personal prosperity—spirit, soul, body. You become secure without fear, filled with confidence and hope. Energy fills your being, and no matter the circumstance, you experience His peace and His rest.

When the word **trust** is used in Scripture, the word *"in"* frequently follows more than 80 times. "In" is the first word in the Bible, indicating that everything starts with God's desire to create a home and family.

By living a life of trust in God, we can answer the question that has challenged mankind for ages:

How do we understand the meaning and purpose of human existence?

Without question, Jesus became man (human flesh) to demonstrate the highest possible life strategy. Jesus revealed a steady stream of information and reality, revealing life at its deepest.

John 1:4—Life was in Him, life that made sense of human existence.

He wants to **occupy** us in a slow process of learning, maturing, and developing our true God-self. You and I are **trustees** of His life within us, and whoever we are and whatever we possess (gifts, talents, abilities, resources) are given to us as a **trust** to be used in the service of His Kingdom on Earth.

"So you must perceive us—not as leaders of factions—but as servants of the Anointed One, those who have been entrusted with God's mysteries. The most important quality of one entrusted with such secrets is that they are faithful and trustworthy" (1 Corinthians 4:1-2 TPT).

Solomon, gifted by God with great wisdom, places two paths before us: trusting in the Lord or trusting in our ability to reason. Trusting God leads to peace, contentment, and good stewardship of our lives.

God is not concerned with perfecting our circumstances but with developing our character, molding us into the person He designed us to become. You will trust someone or something. Only God is worthy of our trust. As human beings, we must trust God and remain faithful even (and especially) when we do not understand the circumstances around us. Letting go and trusting God is the best path and the key to a vibrant and healthy life.

This is well-being in the very depths of our being. **Health** is a wholistic word; it connotes thriving and **radiant wellness—** spiritually, physically, mentally, and financially. In Proverbs, **health** and **healing** are code words for the **total personal provision** that is God's gift to those who walk the wisdom pathway. This alignment with true, Godly reality helps us adopt a true perspective on life. When we genuinely align ourselves with God, His plan, and purpose, we willingly honor Him with our resources and our wealth. What the world needs most is not "love, sweet love," but sons and daughters of God living righteous lives and taking the Kingdom by force. That requires us to present our bodies as a living sacrifice, which means wholeness of spirit, soul, body. We must be submitted to His Lordship and become faithful stewards of all He has given us. The world must see that He is our everything.

Living the Fourth Dimension, living in His Kingdom while on Earth, is how God identified His provision for us. Each of His names tells us something about His provision for us.

Yahweh: I am, I will be
El Shaddai: nurturing God
Adonai: my Lord
Elohim: Ruler, Master, Creator, Sovereign God
Abba: Father, dear Father
Jireh: Provider and provision
Rapha: Healer
Shalom: the Lord is peace

God owns all of our material possessions, and we are simply managing them during our period of Earth stewardship. **Living the Fourth Dimension** is filled with His total abundance. God, the Ruler of that abundance, has granted us favor. Our circumstances never diminish His provision.

"There is an art of living, and the living is excellent only when the self is prepared in all the depths and dimensions of its being." —Plato

Equipped by His Word and His Spirit, we become a people of Godly character and power sent out into our world to manifest His Kingdom. Our greatest danger is putting too little emphasis on His Kingdom message. Though we cannot contain God's fullness, we may receive it to the full measure of our capacity and the degree to which we **yield** to Him. The limitations of our power to transcend ourselves—utilizing powers not yet experienced by us—are yet to be fully known.

And because He has made Himself available to us, to live through us, the laws and provision of His Kingdom mean we can never lack in any area.

Simply put, there is no **higher life strategy** than the one Jesus laid out for us in His Kingdom teachings. When you truly want the highest life, you must choose the **Fourth Dimension.**

When you choose this life, you will take the Kingdom by force.

Keys to Activate Your Kingdom Destiny

Chapter 8

- The Kingdom is actionable, progressive, radical, and powerful—something the world needs to see.

- In the Kingdom, spiritual accomplishments have no limitations or boundaries.

- # 1 law of the Kingdom—the Kingdom rules!

- Total reliance upon God is the doorway into the Kingdom—His rule, reign, and governing power in my daily life.

- Lifestyle and worship are inseparable.

- We have been granted His Power of Attorney to conduct His Kingdom business on Earth.

- In the Kingdom, I experience His personalized Presence.

- In the Kingdom, I discover the life I have lost in my living.

- Always remember I am God-possessed, God-owned, God-controlled, and God-ruled.

- My Kingdom life is not about what happens to me but what happens in and through me.

- Trust is the foundational law of His Kingdom.

- In the Kingdom, Jesus is the actual meaning of life.

Acknowledgments

Over the course of my lifetime, amazingly gifted leaders have spoken great wisdom to me. It would be impossible to list all of their names, but the following have certainly been most notable.

To my mother, Pauline B Scott: a kind, Bible-wise woman, who lived in covenant with God her life.

Dr. Paul L. Walker: a mentor whom I referred to as "the Bishop." He challenged me often.

Floyd Lawhon: a great friend of over 50 years, was like a brother from another mother.

Dr. French Arrington: a Greek scholar, enriched my life with many treasures from the Greek language to expand my Biblical knowledge.

Bill George: a true friend and scholar who helped me write *The Diamond Life* book, and encouraged me to keep writing all these years.

Tom Sterbens: a covenant friend who helps me to keep things real.

Perry Stone: closer than a brother and one of the world's great prophecy minds.

Lester Sumerall: a general in the Kingdom who turned my heart to understanding Kingdom and covenant.

Dr. Tim Hill: a dear friend and a strong, anointed leader in the Kingdom.

Tony Stewart: Kingdom-minded, creative, innovative, and devoted leader with whom I cherish our close bond.

Dr. Jentezen Franklin: a charismatic, national and international leader such as Dr. Billy Graham.

Reverend Sammy Rodriquez: a modern day apostle and prophet with a great Kingdom message and a special friend to me.

Travis Johnson: bold and courageous with a Kingdom anointing for his time.

Phil Cooke: one of the most creative minds, as well as a gifted intellect, and someone who motivates me to greater achievements.

Dr. Jim Garlow: We share in the pain and grief of losing a spouse; he is a great comfort to me.

Chad Connelly: a generational leader, paving the way for revival in government.

Rod Parsley: a pastor to Shirley and me, fiercely dynamic in His Kingdom perspective, and bold as a lion.

Lauren Clark: gifted in writing, challenging me in excellence, hearing my heart, helping me format the books, and pouring her soul into everything we have published—a true covenant friend.

Jenny Schmidt: multi-talented and multi-gifted, intelligent, creative, willing to tackle any project to advance the Kingdom, someone who is a very special friend.

John and Lisa Harris: like family, showing great love, kindness, and generosity to us.

Ed Marroquin: a true son in the Lord, faithful, loyal, a covenant friend.

Bob Billings: a man who truly loves God, loves His Kingdom, and has given much to advance it, always encouraging and praying for me.

Peggy Otieno: faithful servant, encourager, prayer warrior, and a great friend to our family.

Angelica Gongora: a true worshiper, talented, supportive of me and the ministry.

About the Author

Tony Scott is the founding and senior Pastor of theChurch Maumee, with locations in Maumee, Fremont, and online at atthechurch.tv. In 1974, after receiving his BA from Lee University, Tony and his wife ShirleyAnn Scott accepted the pastorate of their first and only church in Sylvania, Ohio, with a congregation of 45 people. The congregation began to grow, and in 2005, theChurch purchased a 57-acre campus.

Their move to the Toledo area was the beginning of a ministry that would reach around the world. As a gifted communicator of biblical principles, he was invited to speak at Christian and business functions with crowds of an excess of 25,000 people. To date, he has spoken in more than ten countries on five continents, relative to living a life of significance.

Tony's desire to write and share powerful Kingdom principles started with his first book, *Living the Diamond Life in a Rocky World*. As they followed their journey, two more books were written by him—*The Increase Life* and *The Diamond Life: You Are More Than You Have Become.* Years passed and *One + One = One: The World's Greatest Love Relationship Equation* was written as a joint effort with his wife, Shirley. Interestingly, unbeknownst to him, she was writing her portion of the book while she fell sick. He wrote his portion and the finished writing their love story after her passing. The book has been a blessing for many marriages and touched many lives.

He was elected to serve on the board of counselors for the International Church of God, with more than 35,000 churches worldwide. For more than 22 years, he served every year he was eligible.

Later, he began a national television ministry that demonstrated a passionate grasp of God's Word and His Spirit. Through His

Kingdom teachings, he has reached thousands of ministry leaders and equipped them to become disciples of Jesus' Kingdom ministry.

The Internship School of Ministry was established by him to train young people for Kingdom service. Several hundred young people graduated from the program and many serve in leadership positions today.

Scott and his wife, ShirleyAnn, experienced oneness of marriage that was both profound and powerful in their ministry. On August 18, 2020, at 4:05 am, Shirley entered in the presence of Jesus, and while she is no longer here physically, she remains with us in spirit and will always be an integral part of theChurch.

For nearly five decades, he has been teaching Biblical principles on how life looks when one pursues the balanced life-spirit, soul, and body-all over the world. Tony continues to pursue His Kingdom assignment and uses his gifts to help others know Jesus.

ONE + ONE = ONE

One + One= One is not just another book about improving your marriage relationship. Actually, it is the very heart of God concerning the most important building block of marriage—oneness. The achievement of this oneness places a shield of protection around your marriage relationship. Live oneness and see marriage as God intended!

ONE + ONE = ONE
INTERACTIVE STUDY GUIDE

This study guide is designed to dig deeper and develop the concepts introduced in the book One + One = One. We designed this book to be used in your home, church, small group studies, and large group studies. We want you to write notes, highlight key points, and interact with your spouse while learning about ONENESS in your marriage relationship.

THE DIAMOND LIFE

Your life is created as a diamond in the rough. The purpose of your life can only be revealed as your experience the Diamond Life Formula. You are to be shaped, cut, chiseled, refined, and polished in order for your true value and beauty to be seen. Read this and become who you really are.

THE INCREASE LIFE

Do you desire genuine increase in the totality of your life? Do you desire to grow in your relationship with God, your Creator and the Provider of all you need? The increase begins within you! The miracle is internal and born of the Holy Spirit residing in you. Get ready for a whole-life transformation of increase!

TO PURCHASE, AND FOR
FREE RESOURCES, VISIT
TONYSCOTT.TV

Made in the USA
Coppell, TX
17 March 2025

47222233R00120